T5-CFQ-504

3 4028 07916 1908
HARRIS COUNTY PUBLIC LIBRARY

813.54 Dep
Depression in Sylvia
Plath's The bell jar

$27.30
ocn744303067
02/09/2012

Social Issues in Literature

Depression
Plath's *The Bell Jar*

Other Books in the Social Issues in Literature Series:

Social Issues in Literature

Depression in Sylvia Plath's *The Bell Jar*

Dedria Bryfonski, Book Editor

GREENHAVEN PRESS
A part of Gale, Cengage Learning

GALE
CENGAGE Learning·

Detroit • New York • San Francisco • New Haven, Conn • Waterville, Maine • London

Elizabeth Des Chenes, *Managing Editor*

© 2012 Greenhaven Press, a part of Gale, Cengage Learning

Gale and Greenhaven Press are registered trademarks used herein under license.

For more information, contact:
Greenhaven Press
27500 Drake Rd.
Farmington Hills, MI 48331-3535
Or you can visit our Internet site at gale.cengage.com

ALL RIGHTS RESERVED.
No part of this work covered by the copyright herein may be reproduced, transmitted, stored, or used in any form or by any means graphic, electronic, or mechanical, including but not limited to photocopying, recording, scanning, digitizing, taping, Web distribution, information networks, or information storage and retrieval systems, except as permitted under Section 107 or 108 of the 1976 United States Copyright Act, without the prior written permission of the publisher.

For product information and technology assistance, contact us at

Gale Customer Support, 1-800-877-4253
For permission to use material from this text or product, submit all requests online at www.cengage.com/permissions

Further permissions questions can be emailed to permissionrequest@cengage.com

Articles in Greenhaven Press anthologies are often edited for length to meet page requirements. In addition, original titles of these works are changed to clearly present the main thesis and to explicitly indicate the author's opinion. Every effort is made to ensure that Greenhaven Press accurately reflects the original intent of the authors. Every effort has been made to trace the owners of copyrighted material.

Cover photograph copyright © Bettmann/Corbis.

LIBRARY OF CONGRESS CATALOGING-IN-PUBLICATION DATA

Depression in Sylvia Plath's The bell jar / Dedria Bryfonski, book editor.
 p. cm. -- (Social issues in literature)
 Includes bibliographical references and index.
 ISBN 978-0-7377-5805-4 (hardcover) -- ISBN 978-0-7377-5806-1 (pbk.)
 1. Plath, Sylvia. Bell jar. 2. Depression, Mental, in literature. I. Bryfonski, Dedria.
 PS3566.L27B4326 2012
 813'.54--dc23
                                                                    2011036480

Printed in the United States of America
 1 2 3 4 5   16 15 14 13 12
ED010

Contents

Chapter 1: Background on Sylvia Plath

   From adolescence, Sylvia Plath struggled with depression,
   eventually giving in to despair and committing suicide at
   age thirty. Her depression was most likely caused by the
   untimely death of her father when she was eight years
   old. Although she was unable to achieve a similar re-
   demption herself, Plath writes of rebirth after despair in
   The Bell Jar and in her poetry.

   Sylvia Plath's poet laureate husband, Ted Hughes, writes
   of the profound connection they shared that shaped the
   writings of both. Although their methods were very different, their "minds soon became two parts of one operation."

   Sylvia Plath struggled in vain for normalcy during her
   time at Cambridge University and successfully concealed
   the tortured side of her existence from her tutor.

   Her former physician concluded that Sylvia Plath's death
   was prompted by depression from an inherited chemical
   imbalance. Her father and several of his family members
   also suffered from depression. Although Plath was under
   treatment for depression, the benefits from her medication would not yet have been effective at the time of her
   death.

Chapter 2: *The Bell Jar* and Depression

Chapter 3: Contemporary Perspectives on Depression

Introduction

At the time of her untimely death at age thirty, Sylvia Plath was a poet just coming into her own voice whose first novel, *The Bell Jar*, had recently been published to moderately favorable reviews. Plath's own tragic story quickly overshadowed her literary output, however, raising her to iconic status and earning *The Bell Jar* comparisons with J.D. Salinger's *The Catcher in the Rye* for its portrayal of a troubled adolescent mind. Critics have found it difficult to separate the author from her work, as Plath drew heavily on her own experiences to create *The Bell Jar*. Plath's battle with depression, suicide attempt, electroshock therapy, feelings of abandonment over losing her father at an early age, and difficulty accepting the limited roles available to women in the 1950s are all material used in her semiautobiographical novel. Because Plath's life and work are so intertwined, an understanding of her life and the era in which she lived add context and provide a deeper understanding of her work.

Critic Linda Wagner-Martin, in *"The Bell Jar": A Novel of the Fifties*, calls the novel "an accurate if frightening view of American life during the 1950s." With the end of World War II, millions of servicemen returned home eager to marry and begin a family. The number of marriages jumped from 1.6 million in 1945 to 2.6 million in 1946, and, predictably, the baby boom began. The population of the United States grew 18.5 percent in the 1950s. Most women found themselves at home, tending to growing families. Virtually the only acceptable roles open to women in the 1950s were those of wife and mother, and the popular culture of the day extolled the happiness and normalcy of the married state for women. Pressure on women to find a suitable husband and marry early was intense.

Sylvia Plath and her alter ego Esther Greenwood were highly intelligent young women who felt stultified in this environment but also felt compelled to succeed according to the terms set by society. Women were expected to be subservient to men, and it was considered unfeminine to be smart and ambitious. Plath felt increasingly torn by the role she aspired to—to be a successful writer—and the role society expected of her—to be a pretty plaything. As Plath's mother wrote in *Letters Home: Correspondence 1950–1963*, "Sylvia was conscious of the prejudice boys built up among themselves about 'brainy' girls. By the time she was a senior in high school, she had learned to hide behind a façade of light-hearted wit when in a mixed group."

To reconcile the conflicting goals of society with her own goals, Plath set impossibly high standards for herself—she wanted to have it all—to be a successful writer while being a wife and mother. As she wrote in *Letters Home*, "I have erected in my mind an image of myself—idealistic and beautiful. Is not that image, free from blemish, the true self—the true perfection? Am I wrong when this image insinuates itself between me and the merciless mirror? . . . Never, never will I reach the perfection I long for with all my soul—my paintings, my poems, my stories—all poor, poor reflections."

Esther Greenwood faces a similar dilemma. Having won a scholarship to be a guest editor at *Ladies Day*, she goes to New York City. As described in *"The Bell Jar"* in *Novels for Students*:

> A brilliant woman with literary aspirations, Esther peers into the future and does not like her choices. She can learn shorthand—as her mother strongly encourages—and land some menial office job after college, or she can marry, live in suburbia, and nurture her husband. What she really wants to do—make a living as a writer—seems unlikely, especially in a profession with so few feminine role models.

Esther faces the same rejection that Plath faced in real life—being turned down for a summer semester creative writing class at Harvard University—and both resort to a suicide attempt in their despair. And in both cases, following botched electroshock therapy, both Esther and Plath rebound from depression with the help of a sympathetic therapist. There Esther's story ends, but Plath's continues.

In the decade following her suicide attempt, Plath managed to have it all—to have a successful academic career at Cambridge; marry the noted poet Ted Hughes; bear two children; teach English at her alma mater, Smith College; and write prolifically and with a developing maturity. To her friends and acquaintances, she seemed utterly normal. Of her early years in London, her friend A. Alvarez writes, "In those days Sylvia seemed effaced, the poet taking a back seat to the young mother and housewife." With the birth of her first child and the publication of her first book of poetry, Plath seemed to grow into her own. According to Alvarez, by June 1962, "Sylvia had changed. No longer quiet and withheld, a housewifely appendage to a powerful husband, she seemed made solid and complete, her own woman again." Plath's biographer, Eileen M. Aird, writes: "Although writing was now taking up a great deal of her time Sylvia Plath was also a wife and mother; she did housework and gardening with enthusiasm and cared for her daughter efficiently and well as she did everything."

Yet lurking under her placid demeanor was a predisposition toward depression that was probably inherited, according to her doctor, John Horder. In patients with such an inherited link, stressful events can trigger a severe depression that, if not treated in time, can result in suicide. Plath was coping with the desertion of her husband for another woman, the severe cold of a London winter, and caring for two small children. The drug she was prescribed for her depression required almost two weeks to be effective. At the time of her death she had been taking it for only a few days. In the parlance of her novel, the bell jar descended.

Her tutor and mentor, Dorothea Krook, professed shock at Plath's suicide:

> She had seemed to me, as I have said, a creature breathing only spiritual health, vitality, and resilience; to discover that there was also a pathological element to take account of taxed my imagination beyond its resources. Like everyone who loved her, I have brooded a great deal about this dark, death-enchanted side of her, trying to understand it, failing each time I tried.

Although *The Bell Jar* is set in the 1950s, its theme of how the strictures of society can damage a sensitive young person remains relevant today. In *Social Issues in Literature: Depression in Sylvia Plath's* The Bell Jar critics and commentators examine depression in the novel as well as some perspectives on depression in young people today.

Chronology

1932
Sylvia Plath is born on October 27 in Boston, the first child of Aurelia Schober Plath and Otto Emil Plath.

1935
Sylvia's younger brother, Warren, is born on April 27.

1936
The Plath family moves to Winthrop, Massachusetts.

1938
Plath begins public school in Winthrop in September.

1940
Otto Plath dies on November 5.

1942
The Plath family moves to Wellesley, Massachusetts, and Aurelia Plath begins teaching at Boston University. The two Plath children enter Marshall Perrin Grammar School.

1944
Plath enters Alice L. Phillips Junior High School and writes for the school's literary magazine, the *Phillipian*.

1947
Plath enters Gamaliel Bradford Senior High School in September.

1950
Plath graduates from high school and receives a full scholarship to Smith College. *Seventeen* magazine publishes her short story "And Summer Will Not Come Again," and the *Christian Science Monitor* publishes "Bitter Strawberries," a poem.

1953

Plath spends her summer in New York as a guest editor for *Mademoiselle*. Returning home to Wellesley, she suffers severe depression, receives electroshock treatments, and attempts suicide. She is treated at McLean Hospital in Belmont, Massachusetts.

1954

Plath returns to Smith College and receives a scholarship to a summer program at Harvard University.

1955

Plath graduates summa cum laude from Smith and is awarded a Fulbright scholarship to attend Cambridge University in England.

1956

Plath meets poet Ted Hughes on February 25 and marries him secretly on June 16.

1957

Plath and Hughes move to Massachusetts, where Plath teaches English at Smith College.

1958

Hughes gets a part-time teaching position at the University of Massachusetts at Amherst. The couple conclude that teaching and poetry are incompatible, quit their teaching posts, and move to Boston. Plath takes part-time jobs and resumes therapy.

1959

Hughes and Plath return to England in December.

1960

Hughes and Plath take a flat in London. Their daughter, Frieda Rebecca Hughes, is born April 1. Plath's book of poetry *The Colossus* is published in October.

1961

Plath has a miscarriage and an appendectomy. In July she and Hughes buy a house in Devon, England. Plath finishes writing *The Bell Jar* in August.

1962

Son Nicholas Farrar Hughes is born January 17. Hughes commits adultery, leaves Plath and the children, and moves to London. Plath works on the poetry that would be published in *Ariel* and *Winter Trees* and moves with her children to a London flat in December.

1963

London experiences an unusually cold winter. *The Bell Jar* is published in England on January 14 under the pseudonym Victoria Lucas. Plath commits suicide by gas from the oven on the morning of February 11.

1965

Hughes publishes his edition of the *Ariel* poems.

1969

Assia Wevill, the lover Hughes left Plath for, commits suicide, also killing the child Hughes fathered.

1970

Hughes marries Carol Orchard.

1971

Hughes publishes *Crossing the Water* and *Winter Trees*, collections from Plath's unpublished work.

1971

The Bell Jar is published in the United States.

1977

Hughes publishes *Johnny Panic and the Bible of Dreams and Other Prose Writing*, Plath's stories, essays, and some journal excerpts.

1981

Hughes edits and publishes *Sylvia Plath: The Collected Poems*, which wins a Pulitzer Prize for Poetry in 1982.

1982

Hughes publishes *The Journals of Sylvia Plath, 1950–1962* and admits that he destroyed Plath's last journal.

1983

Hughes is named Poet Laureate of the United Kingdom.

1998

Hughes's last poetic work, *Birthday Letters*, describes his relationship with Plath.

Background on
Sylvia Plath

The Life of Sylvia Plath

Timothy Materer

Timothy Materer is a professor in the Department of English at the University of Missouri. He is the author of numerous books and articles on literature, including James Merrill's Apocalypse.

Sylvia Plath was a complex person and artist whose persona has been interpreted in different ways by literary critics, states Materer in the following viewpoint. The circumstances of her life and death have made her a mythic figure, he suggests, making it hard to separate the woman from her best-known work, the semiautobiographical novel The Bell Jar. *Although the heroine of* The Bell Jar *conquers her depression and is reborn, Plath herself was unable to exorcise her demons and took her own life, robbing the literary world of a gifted poet and novelist.*

In his introduction to *The Journals of Sylvia Plath, 1950–62,* her husband, poet Ted Hughes, wrote that she wore "many masks" but that he believes he knew her "real self"—"the self I had married, after all, and lived with and knew well." Yet this claim is as controversial as her biographers' claims to have given accurate accounts of her life. The controversy began soon after her suicide in 1963, when Hughes threatened a London magazine with legal action if it published the second part of A. Alvarez's account of the suicide. This incident set the tone for further dealings between the Plath estate and her biographers, who often complain that Hughes will tolerate only his version of the "real" Sylvia Plath. . . .

Plath's Life and Art Were Intertwined

The estate's strict control of copyright and its editing of such writings as Plath's journals and letters have caused the most

Timothy Materer, "Sylvia Plath," in *American Novelists Since World War II: Fourth Series, Dictionary of Literary Biography*, ed. James R. Giles and Wanda H. Giles. Andover, UK: 1995. www.cengage.com/permissions. Copyright © 1995 by Gale, a part of Cengage Learning, Inc. All rights reserved. Reproduced by permission.

serious problems for scholars. Yet even without these obstacles to interpretation Plath's identity would seem mysterious. Her life seems mythical rather than historical because she herself made her life the substance of her art. Her constant theme, the transformation and rebirth of the self, has given her readers multiple and sometimes contradictory versions of that self. Her critics have viewed her, for example, as the tragic victim of a childhood trauma when her father died and of an equally painful abandonment when her husband left her shortly before her death. Less-sympathetic critics have characterized her as the product of a generation of women who wanted too much: a perfect husband, home, and family as well as an independent career. Some view her as a feminist ahead of her time in fighting for a woman's independent identity. Perhaps the best-known persona is Plath the confessional poet whose "muse was rage," as Diane Middlebrook has said in "The Enraged Muse", and who finally expressed that rage in *The Bell Jar*, her only novel, and *Ariel*.

Her Father's Death Caused Plath's Depression

Plath's contradictory personality emerged from what at first seems an uncomplicated and conventional American background. Although her father died when she was a child, Plath's family life was otherwise comfortable. By the time she was a scholarship student at Smith College she was a popular, physically active, and talented young woman who won many prizes for her academic and creative achievements. As a graduate student she attended Cambridge University and married a brilliant English poet, Hughes, with whom she had two children, Nicholas and Frieda. Despite this record of achievements, she struggled continually against severe depression from at least her junior year of college—the same year that the autobiographical narrative of *The Bell Jar* begins. Although the depressed periods were matched by those of elation and creativity, the oscillation between these extremes was exhausting. She wrote in her journal for 20 June 1958, "it is as if my life were magically run by two electric currents: joyous positive and despairing negative—which ever is running at the moment dominates my life, floods it." As both her poetry and fiction suggest, her depression was related to the death of her father.

Otto Emil Plath was born in Germany in 1885 and came to America in 1900. By 1922 he was an instructor of German and then of biology at Boston University. Her mother, Aurelia Schober Plath, twenty-one years younger than her father, was his student in 1929. After Aurelia had graduated and was teaching high school, they married in January 1932. He insisted that his new wife quit her job and assist him in his research and in rewriting his dissertation, published as *Bumblebees and Their Ways.* Sylvia was born in the Jamaica Plain section of Boston on 27 October 1932; her brother, Warren, was born in 1935. From 1935 on their father's health was poor, but he stubbornly refused to see a doctor, fearing that he would only learn he had cancer. (Plath later speculated that his refusal to do so was suicidal.) He steadily declined until he collapsed in 1940 from the effects of untreated diabetes. After an operation to amputate his leg in October 1940, he suffered an embolism and died on 5 November 1940. The eight-year-old Plath's response when her mother broke the news of her father's death was to say that she would never speak to God again. Thinking the children were too young, Mrs. Plath did not let them attend the funeral. They moved from their house near the ocean, which Plath missed deeply, to Wellesley, Massachusetts, in 1942. She recalled her love of the ocean in her essay "Ocean 1212-W", collected in *Johnny Panic and the Bible of Dreams and Other Prose Writings*:

My childhood landscape was not land but the end of the land—the cold, salt, running hills of the Atlantic. I sometimes think my vision of the sea is the clearest thing I.

own . . . When I was learning to creep, my mother set me down on the beach to see what I thought of it. I crawled straight for the coming wave and was just through the wall of green when she caught my heels.

Her memories of moving away from the sea are briefly expressed: "My father died, we moved inland. Whereon those nine first years of my life sealed themselves off like a ship in a bottle—beautiful, inaccessible, obsolete, a fine, white flying myth."

After the move to Wellesley, Aurelia Plath resumed her academic career with an appointment at Boston University to develop and teach in a program for training medical secretaries. Plath entered Smith College on a scholarship in 1950. Intent on academic and social success, she pushed herself so hard during her college years that a pattern of colds and sinus infections at times of stress developed, which also became characteristic of her adult life. These illnesses in turn aggravated her recurrent depressions. In an entry of her journal for 20 February 1952 she confessed, "Small problems, mentions of someone else's felicity, evidence of someone else's talents frightened me, making me react hollowly, fighting jealousy, envy, hate."

Plath Attempts Suicide

In 1952 Plath won a five-hundred-dollar first prize for fiction from *Mademoiselle*. The next summer she was awarded a student editorship on *Mademoiselle* and spent June working in New York, an experience that provided the material for the first chapters of *The Bell Jar*. Her anxiety to excel at whatever she did made her frenetic stay in New York particularly hard because she was competing with other outstanding, prizewinning young women. Returning home, the news that she had not been accepted in Frank O'Connor's short-story course at Harvard University further depressed her, and she was placed in the care of a doctor who prescribed electroshock treatments on an outpatient basis. The electroshocks, a drastic though not uncommon therapy at the time, were poorly administered and increased rather than relieved her anxieties. On 24 August 1953 she hid herself in the cellar of her home after taking about forty sleeping pills, prescribed for her, from a locked metal box where her mother kept them. She swallowed them and was found two days later when her brother heard her moans, and after her physical recovery she was admitted to the Massachusetts General Hospital (where poets Robert Lowell and Anne Sexton would also be patients) under the care of a competent psychiatrist, Dr. Ruth Beuscher. Although Beuscher also used electrotherapy, she won Plath's trust and was the model for Dr. Nolan in *The Bell Jar*. In the novel Dr. Nolan helps her patient foster the independence that allows her to face the hospital's examining board successfully and return to her life.

Similarly, Plath returned to college in the spring of 1954 (at first under special supervision), completed her honors thesis on the motif of the double in the work of Fyodor Dostoyevsky, and graduated summa cum laude in 1955. She received a Fulbright grant and in October began her studies at Newnham College, Cambridge, England.

Plath Marries Ted Hughes

In Cambridge she met Hughes, whose poetry she already admired. In her journal for 5 May 1958 she remembered her first impression of his poems: "tough, knotty, blazing with color and fury, most eminently sayable." She described him in one of the letters collected in *Letters Home: Correspondence, 1950–63* as the "strongest man in the world," someone who commanded attention "like a blast of Jove's lightning." Their first meeting in a Cambridge pub in February 1956 was dramatic. Hughes snatched her hairband and earrings to keep as mementos, and Plath, to show that she also had a passionate nature, drew blood by biting his cheek. Their relationship developed as they met in London and Cambridge, and they married on 16 June 1956 and honeymooned in Spain. After Plath took her Cambridge exams for the B.A. degree they came to America, where Plath began teaching at Smith College. Typing his poems and sending them to periodicals and contests, she delighted to see his career thrive, but her own career languished. She felt inadequate as a teacher and found preparing for classes too stressful and time-consuming. She wrote in her journal for 8 March 1958, "I am living and teaching on rereadings, on notes of other people, sour as heartburn, between two unachieved shapes: between the original teacher and the original writer: neither." They moved to Boston in 1958 and tried to live on their income as writers; Plath, however, took part-time jobs to help with their finances. A secretarial job at the Massachusetts General Hospital gave her the background for her best short story, "Johnny Panic and the Bible of Dreams", which also dealt with her traumatic memories of electroshock. She also attended Lowell's writing seminar at Boston University in 1958, where she became friendly with Sexton, and resumed treatments with Dr. Beuscher to cope with her recurrent depression. Despite the publication of her poems in magazines such as the *Nation, London Magazine,* and *The New Yorker,* her depressions centered on her low productivity, publishers' rejections of the manuscript that would eventually develop into *The Colossus,* and her inability to make progress on a novel. After a summer touring and two months at the Yaddo writing colony, in December 1959 the Hugheses returned to England, where they hoped to live more cheaply as they advanced their careers.

Their first year in England was by all appearances successful. Plath gave birth to a daughter, Frieda Rebecca, in April 1960, and in October her much-revised first volume of poetry was published as *The Colossus,* a reference to her father as an "oracle" or "[m]outhpiece of the dead" that suggests she was finding her true inspiration through exploring her past. Although reviews of *The Colossus* were generally favorable, they were few. . . .

The Bell Jar Is Published in England

In 1961 she made a new start on novel writing, which unlike poetry writing allowed her to write regularly as she carried out her household responsibilities. Despite a miscarriage and an appendectomy in 1961, she finished *The Bell Jar* in August. In the same month they bought a house in North Tawton, Devon, where their second child, Nicholas Farrar, was born in January 1962. During this time she wrote some of her finest poems, including "Blackberrying", "The Moon and the Yew Tree", "Little Fugue", and the long poem "Three Women". This period ended when she learned in July 1962 of Hughes's affair with another woman. The shock of this revelation is described in her poem "Words Heard, By Accident, Over the Phone", where the voice of the other woman is as "[t]hick as foreign coffee, and with a sluggy pulse." After she and Hughes failed at an attempt at reconciliation, she moved with her two children into a London flat that once had been occupied by William Butler Yeats. Depressed by the separation, the hardships of a severe winter, and continual respiratory illnesses, she wrote the bitter poems that first appeared in *Ariel*. She wrote her mother on 16 October 1962, during a month when she wrote some thirty poems, "I am writing the best poems of my life; they will make my name."

In January *The Bell Jar* was published in England under the pseudonym Victoria Lucas. Although she told her brother that her novel was "a pot-boiler and no one must read it," she must have known that its harsh biographical portraits would soon come to her family's attention. Indeed, her mother tried to discourage Hughes from allowing its publication in America. The theme of *The Bell Jar*, and of the manuscript version of *Ariel* before Hughes rearranged it following her death, was rebirth after a period of suffering and despair. Yet on 11 February Plath committed suicide by inhaling gas from her kitchen oven. Questions that arose at the time, such as whether she hoped that someone would also discover this suicide attempt in time to stop it and whether she left a suicide note, have remained unanswered. . . .

The Bell Jar Is Semiautobiographical

The Bell Jar is a finely plotted novel full of vivid characters and written in the astringent but engaging style one expects from a poet as frank and observant as Plath. The atmosphere of hospitals and sickness, of incidents of bleeding and electrocution, set against images of confinement and liberation, unify the novel's imagery. Liberation is often associated with the sea; for example, the happiest memory of Esther Greenwood, the main character, is being with her father on a sunny beach. Death seems to her a "sweeping tide, rush[ing] me to sleep," but the sea is also life-giving: "the water had spat me up into the sun, the world was sparkling all about me like blue and green and yellow semi-precious stones." The novel's major image is the bell jar in which Esther must breathe her "own sour air." This image is augmented by other images of confinement, such as boxes, cages, prison rooms, or vans, and the medical school's "big glass bottles full of babies that had died before they were born."

The plot of *The Bell Jar* closely follows the events of Plath's own life in 1953–1954. The New York chapters (chapters 1–9) lead to a second section (chapters 10–13), which concerns her breakdown and suicide attempts; the third and final section (chapters 14–20) describes the development of a new, independent self. The novel's tone is set as Esther, nineteen years old, agonizes over newspaper stories about the death by electrocution of Julius and Ethel Rosenberg on charges of spying. The heat of New York and her fashionable new clothes make her as uncomfortable as her relationships with her colleagues and her career-woman boss. . . .

The book's macabre humor is evident as, with the application of a good student, she explores the efficacy of suicide methods of shooting, drowning, hanging, and slashing her wrists. She tries to drown herself twice, but the first time, when she feels the ocean's "mortal ache," her "flesh winced, in cowardice, from such a death." The second time the water is warmer: "I fanned myself down, but before I knew where I was, the water had spat me up into the sun." When she tries to hang herself, she discovers that she is "poor at knots" and that her house has the "wrong kind of ceilings." She therefore walks through the house, "the silk cord dangling from my neck like a yellow cat's tail and finding no place to fasten it." Esther finally chooses the unreliable method of swallowing sleeping pills in exactly the manner Plath did during her own life. . . .

The Bell Jar concludes with a spiritual rebirth in the protagonist that Plath herself could not achieve in 1963. When she died she had written some of the finest lyrics in modern English-language poetry. She had also completed a draft of a second novel, "Double Exposure" (Hughes said the manuscript disappeared in 1970), that may have promised an achievement in fiction to match hers in poetry. She was the mother of two bright, healthy children and was forming new friendships in London, yet the fullness of her life could not hold back the tides of depression. In one of her last poems— "Words", dated 1 February 1963—she wrote of the fatality of such recurrent and despairing moods:

> Words dry and riderless. . . . From the bottom of the pool, fixed stars Govern a life.

Sylvia Plath Was the Personification of American Literature

Ted Hughes, as told to Drue Heinz

Ted Hughes was Poet Laureate of the United Kingdom from 1984 until his death in 1998 and is considered to be one of the finest poets of his generation. Hughes was also a literary critic, translator, and author of children's books. He was married to Sylvia Plath from 1956 until their separation in 1963, shortly before Plath commited suicide. Drue Heinz is the former publisher of the Paris Review *and a well-known patron of the arts.*

In the following viewpoint, Hughes describes his relationship with Plath and defends his decision to destroy the journal she kept during her last months. Although he and Plath had different literary influences and employed different methods, Hughes claims their "minds soon became two parts of one operation" as they "dreamed a lot of shared or complementary dreams." He burned her last sad journal, he says, because he did not want their children to read it.

*D*rue Heinz: Could you talk a bit . . . about Sylvia?

Ted Hughes: Sylvia and I met because she was curious about my group of friends at university and I was curious about her. I was working in London but I used to go back up to Cambridge at weekends. Half a dozen or so of us made a poetic gang. Our main cooperative activity was drinking in the Anchor and our main common interest, apart from fellow

Ted Hughes, interviewed by Drue Heinz, "The Art of Poetry, No. 71," *Paris Review*, no. 134, Spring 1995, pp. 19–56. Copyright © 1995 by The Paris Review and the Estate of Ted Hughes. All rights reserved. Reproduced by permission of the Wylie Agency LLC and Faber and Faber LTD.

feeling and mutual attraction, was Irish, Scottish, and Welsh traditional songs—folk songs and broadsheet ballads. We sang a lot. Recorded folk songs were rare in those days. Our poetic interests were more mutually understood than talked about. But we did print a broadsheet [newspaper] of literary comment. In one issue, one of our group, our Welshman, Dan Huws, demolished a poem that Sylvia had published, "Caryatids." He later became a close friend of hers, wrote a beautiful elegy when she died. That attack attracted her attention. Also, she had met one of our group, Lucas Myers, an American, who was an especially close friend of mine. Luke was very dark and skinny. He could be incredibly wild. Just what you hoped for from Tennessee. His poems were startling to us— Hart Crane, Wallace Stevens vocabulary, zany. He interested Sylvia. In her journals she records the occasional dream in which Luke appears unmistakably. When we published a magazine full of our own poems, the only issue of St. Botolph's, and launched it at a big dance party, Sylvia came to see what the rest of us looked like. Up to that point I'd never set eyes on her. I'd heard plenty about her from an English girlfriend who shared supervisions with her. There she suddenly was, raving Luke's verses at Luke and my verses at me.

Once I got to know her and read her poems, I saw straight off that she was a genius of some kind. Quite suddenly we were completely committed to each other and to each other's writing. The year before, I had started writing again after the years of the devastation of university. I'd just written what have become some of my more anthologized pieces—"The Thought Fox," the Jaguar poems, "Wind." I see now that when we met, my writing, like hers, left its old path and started to circle and search. To me, of course, she was not only herself— she was America and American literature in person. I don't know what I was to her. Apart from the more monumental classics—[Leo] Tolstoy [Fyodor] Dostoyevsky, and so on—my background reading was utterly different from hers. But our minds soon became two parts of one operation. We dreamed a lot of shared or complementary dreams. Our telepathy was intrusive. I don't know whether our verse exchanged much, if we influenced one another that way—not in the early days. Maybe others see that differently. Our methods were not the same. Hers was to collect a heap of vivid objects and good words and make a pattern; the pattern would be projected from somewhere deep inside, from her very distinctly evolved myth. It appears distinctly evolved to a reader now—despite having been totally unconscious to her then. My method was to find a thread end and draw the rest out of a hidden tangle. Her method was more painterly, mine more narrative, perhaps. Throughout our time together we looked at each other's verses at every stage—up to the Ariel poems of October 1962, which was when we separated.

Plath's Journals Were Material for a Novel

Do you know how Sylvia used her journals? Were they diaries or notebooks for her poetry and fiction?

Well, I think Janet Malcolm in *The New Yorker* made a fair point about the journals: a lot of what's in them is practice . . . shaping up for some possible novel, little chapters for novels. She was constantly sketching something that happened and working it into something she thought might fit into a novel. She thought of her journals as working notes for some ultimate novel although, in fact, I don't think any of it ever went into *The Bell Jar*. She changed certain things to make them work, to make some kind of symbolic statement of a feeling. She wasn't writing an account of this or that event; she was trying to get to some other kind of ancient, i.e., childhood, material. Some of her short stories take the technique a stage further. Wanting to express that ancient feeling.

What happened to Plath's last novel that was never published?

Sylvia Plath and her husband, the English poet Ted Hughes, on their honeymoon in Paris in 1956. © Photo Researchers.

Well, what I was aware of was a fragment of a novel, about seventy pages. Her mother said she saw a whole novel, but I never knew about it. What I was aware of was sixty, seventy pages that disappeared. And to tell you the truth, I always assumed her mother took them all on one of her visits.

Would you talk about burning Plath's journals?

What I actually destroyed was one journal that covered maybe two or three months, the last months. And it was just sad. I just didn't want her children to see it, no. Particularly her last days.

Hughes Defends His Decision to Reedit *Ariel*

What about Ariel? Did you reorder the poems there?

Well, nobody in the U.S. wanted to publish the collection as she left it. The one publisher over there who was interested wanted to cut it to twenty poems. The fear seemed to be that the whole lot might provoke some sort of backlash—some revulsion. And at the time, you know, few magazine editors would publish the Ariel poems; few liked them. The qualities weren't so obvious in those days. So right from the start there was a question over just how the book was to be presented. I wanted the book that would display the whole range and variety. I remember writing to the man who suggested cutting it to twenty—a longish intemperate letter, as I recall—and saying I felt that was simply impossible. I was torn between cutting some things out and putting some more things in. I was keen to get some of the last poems in. But the real problem was, as I've said, that the U.S. publishers I approached did not want Sylvia's collection as it stood. Faber in England were happy to publish the book in any form. Finally it was a compromise—I cut some things out and I put others in. As a result I have been mightily accused of disordering her intentions and even suppressing part of her work. But those charges have evolved twenty, thirty years after the event. They are based on simple ignorance of how it all happened. Within six years of that first publication all her late poems were published in collections—all that she'd put in her own Ariel and those she'd kept out. It was her growing frame, of course, that made it possible to publish them. And years ago, for anybody who was curious, I published the contents and order of her own typescript—so if anybody wants to see what her Ariel was it's quite easy. On the other hand, how final was her order? She was forever shuffling the poems in her typescripts—looking for different connections, better sequences. She knew there were always new possibilities, all fluid.

Sylvia Plath Was a Shining Intellect and a Superb Student

Dorothea Krook

Dorothea Krook was a Latvian-born English literary scholar who taught literature at Cambridge University, Hebrew University, and Tel Aviv University. She is the author of The Ordeal of Consciousness in Henry James *and* The Elements of Tragedy. *While teaching at Cambridge, Krook was tutor to Sylvia Plath and is considered an important role model for the poet and novelist.*

In the following viewpoint, Krook reflects on her association with Plath, calling her one of the most responsive pupils she ever taught. In her attempt to be normal, Plath hid the destructive side of her personality from her tutor, Krook writes. It was only after reading The Bell Jar, Ariel, *and* A. Alvarez's account *of Plath's death that Krook came to know the personal demons Plath was fighting.*

As I was reading the poem "Daddy" for the first time, I suddenly recalled my earliest impression of Sylvia Plath, before I knew who she was. It was at the opening lecture of my course on Henry James, at the beginning of the Michaelmas Term [i.e., September 29, St. Michael's Day], 1955, Sylvia's first year at Cambridge. I had walked into the Mill Lane lecture room a few minutes early, and was gazing idly at my new audience, observing that it was small and probably wondering whether it was also choice. As I gazed, I noticed a conspicuously tall girl standing in one of the aisles, facing toward me, and staring at me intently. I was struck by the concentrated intensity of her scrutiny, which gave her face an ugly, almost

Dorothea Krook, "Recollections of Sylvia Plath," in *Sylvia Plath: Method and Madness*, ed. Edward Butscher. Tuscon, AZ: Schaffner Press, 1976, pp. 49–60. Copyright © 1976 by Schaffner Press. All rights reserved. Reproduced by permission.

coarse, expression, accentuated by the extreme redness of her heavily painted mouth and its downward turn at the corners. I distinctly remember wondering whether she was Jewish. This was a thought that could not have occurred to me more than half a dozen times in all my thirteen years at Cambridge; one somehow never wondered whether people were or were not Jewish, unless presumably the Jewish marks were especially prominent. The tall girl with the face distorted by the intensity of her interest, curiosity, whatever it was, must have seemed to me to show the marks in this way, or I cannot imagine why the thought should have crossed my mind. I have remembered it often since, with the strangest emotions, as more and more has come to be known about her passionate feeling for Jews and her sense of belonging with them.

Plath Appeared Serene as a Student

I never again, literally never, saw that expression on Sylvia's face in all the time I knew her at Cambridge. Only when at the time of her death the London *Observer* published a picture of her, along with [A.] Alvarez's moving notice, I seemed to catch a glimpse of it again, in the wildly, feverishly staring eyes of that dreadful unfamiliar face, the desperate-defiant look in the eye somehow intensified by the distaff of unkept hair hanging about her shoulders.

There was nothing wild, feverish or defiant, and nothing unkept, about the Sylvia Plath who came to me for supervision on the English Moralists from the second or third term of that year 1955/56. I see her clearly at this moment before my mind's eye, sitting on the sofa in my small sitting-room at 111 Grantchester Meadows: always neat and fresh, wearing charming, girlish clothes, the kind of clothes that made you look at the girl, not the garments; hair down to the shoulders still, but ever so neatly brushed and combed, and held back in place by a broad bandeau on the crown. I remember the bandeau because I think I never saw her without it; my first irrelevant thought as I stared, stupefied, at the picture in the *Observer* was "Where is the bandeau? It *can't* be her—she's not wearing her bandeau." This charming American neatness and freshness is what I chiefly recall about her physical person, even more than her beauty; though she was of course beautiful, as Wendy Campbell says, as we must have said to each other often enough. She seemed also, I remember, less tall than she was, because she did not hold herself in a tall girl's way: always straight and graceful, but somehow humble at the same time, which had the effect of diminishing her physical height.

This effect was produced even more by the typical expression of her face. Eager and mobile, tranquil and serene, all at once: I never saw her face express anything else in the many long supervision hours we spent together. I did not think of her as one of my most "brilliant" pupils (I shall return to this point); I thought of her rather as one of the most deeply, movingly, responsive pupils I had ever had. I felt the things I said, we said, her authors said, mattered to her in an intimate way, answering to intense personal needs, reaching to depths of her spirit to which I had no direct access (and didn't mind not having, being satisfied with the visible effects).

Plath Was an "A" Student

As every teacher knows, there is no greater inspiration to letting oneself go intellectually than is this rare kind of receptiveness in a pupil. I did let myself go with Sylvia, as I have done I think with no more than five or six others in a teaching career of nearly thirty years. It was a matter of spreading one's wings to the argument, as Plato says, letting it lead whither it will. Plato was indeed the central figure in our discussions; we seemed to linger on and on over Plato, doubtless at the expense of the other Moralists; but this was something that often happened with my best pupils, usually with no regrets afterward. Some time during the period Sylvia was coming to me for supervision, Miss Mary Ellen Chase of Smith College, Sylvia's special sponsor and friend, came on a visit to Cambridge, and reported amusingly on Sylvia's enthusiasm about her Plato studies. "She talks about *nothing* else," said Miss Chase, with much pretended exasperation, "Plato and Mrs. Krook, Mrs. Krook and Plato, Mrs. Krook on Plato, Plato on Mrs. Krook . . . It's hard to know *which* she's talking about, whether it's Plato or Mrs. Krook she admires most . . ." I remember how we laughed about this at the dinner party at the Garden House Hotel, and how touched and flattered I was by this confirmation of my own feeling that Sylvia was greatly enjoying our Plato sessions.

I have racked my memory to recall what were some of the particular things I said to Sylvia or she to me about Plato and the rest. But I can remember nothing: not a single utterance. All that comes back to me is a general vision, clear and pure like the golden light of the Platonic world we had appropriated, of an extraordinarily happy freedom of communication. Love and beauty in the *Symposium*, justice in the *Republic*, the pleasant and the good in the *Gorgias*, knowledge and opinion in the *Meno*, the contemplative intelligence, the practical intelligence, the Platonic rationalism, the Platonic mysticism: these must have been some of the great topics we entered into and lost ourselves in. I remember that I pursued them with her further than I had done with any other student, drawing out implications, soaring into generalizations, reviewing my personal life's experience for illustration or proof, in a way I usually reserved only for my soul's most secret conversation with itself. The light of participation in Sylvia's eyes, shining so it seemed to me with understanding and delight, is one of the sweetest, most imperishable memories of my teaching life.

She wrote for me, almost every week, an excellent paper: long, full, cogently argued, carefully written—everything that goes to make an *alpha* paper. She got her alphas, and I praised the papers as they deserved; yet somewhere in the subconscious depths of my mind there was a reservation. I think I would have expressed it at the time (if I had attempted to express it, which I didn't) as a sense of their somehow, nevertheless, not penetrating all the way: neither to the depths of the subject, nor (more important) to the depths of her own experience. It seems this did happen in our oral communications, our joint explorations; it did not happen, in quite the same way, in her own independent grapplings with her authors; and it never occurred to me what the reason might be, that "criticism" was not for her the most natural, congenial mode of self-articulation. What I registered was only a sense of her seeming to hold off a little from her subject, not wholly surrendering herself to it; and of holding back something, perhaps a great deal, of herself. All unconsciously, of course; her conscious aim, clearly, was to put all she knew, give all she had, to her weekly academic exercises. Indeed (I remember this, too, as a distinct impression, though barely expressed at the time), I felt in her a certain strain or tension about these essays: arising from an anxiety (I supposed) to "do them well," to excel, to distinguish herself; and not just now and then, but consistently, without lapse. Of course I applauded this fine noncompetitive ambition; what teacher in his senses would not? But it contributed to the reservation which made me think of her as an excellent, not a brilliant, student; though I am sure I must have spoken of her as "brilliant" often enough, in the loose way one does in speaking of one's best students when one is in no mood for fine distinctions.

Plath Disguised Her Struggle for Normalcy

In this connection, I recall that the only hint I ever had about a more flamboyant "past" in Sylvia's life was something I heard about her first two terms at Cambridge, before she started coming to me for supervision. I don't think it was from Sylvia herself that I had it; it may have been from Wendy, or from someone else. What I heard gave me a vague picture of Sylvia

Undated photo of Sylvia Plath. © Bettmann/Corbis.

during that time leading an intensely social life, writing or contributing to a woman's page in the undergraduate magazine *Granta*, involved in stage activities (Cambridge was a great place for amateur theatre), and being very popular and sought after. By the end of her second term, she had decided that all this was a "waste of time" (I seem to remember my informant using this phrase), that she must put it aside to concentrate on her studies, lead a serious, responsible life without frivolous distractions, and so on. I remember being amused at the fervor of the renunciation. She was not after all the first person who had succumbed to the glamour of Cambridge in her first few terms; I had had the experience myself in a mild form in my first year at Cambridge, when scarcely older than Sylvia I had come to Newnham as a research student; and I had learnt since that newcomers from outside (America, South Africa, or wherever) were particularly susceptible. I also felt, in a dim way, that her uneasy conscience about her first "wasted" terms, her self-reforming zeal, her desire to live down, live away, these passages in her recent past had something to do with the strenuous note I seemed to detect in her seriousness about her studies and her weekly essays. I didn't know anything about her life as a student in America; and I knew nothing, of course, about *The Bell Jar*.

Reviewing these remembered impressions or intuitions in the light of later knowledge, I have come to see in them meanings of which I had no inkling at the time. When after her death I read the poems in the *Ariel* volume, and more recently *Winter Trees*, I thought I could see why I had felt that those long, full, excellent essays on the English Moralists did not reach down to her innermost being. And since the apppearance of *The Bell Jar* and Alvarez's account of her death, I have seemed to recognize in her whole academic effort at Cambridge a great, perhaps even a titanic, struggle for "normalcy" against the forces of disintegration within her. I knew nothing about these forces; but she, poor doomed girl, did; and I now believe that she may well have resolved, consciously and deliberately, to defeat them once and for all and save herself from destruction by the path Cambridge had opened up to her. To be a successful teacher of English Literature at Smith College (she might have argued to herself) is one obvious way of being "normal"; therefore, she must bend all her efforts to qualify herself for this saving normality; therefore, she must write excellent, the best possible, essays for me, get a First in the Tripos [final exam], and so on. I don't mean, of course, that her passionate interest in her studies was not genuine; I only mean that her secret fight against disintegration was a powerful additional motive for the interest and the passion. . . .

Plath Was Passionately Happy with Ted Hughes

The more personal side of our friendship developed, I seem to recall, from the time of her marriage to Ted Hughes. I became involved in this for reasons serious enough for Sylvia at the start, though in the end amusing as well. At the beginning of the Michaelmas term 1956, her second year at Cambridge, Sylvia appeared, extremely agitated, to tell me that she had "secretly" married Ted during the long vacation, that they had had a marvelous summer in Spain, ecstatically happy, wonderfully productive—happy, obviously, because they adored each other, productive because (she said) they had both managed to write a great deal. But now the hour of reckoning had come: she had got married without tutorial permission, and had up to now kept it from tutorial knowledge (this is what she had meant by saying she had done it "secretly," which I had at first not understood), she was afraid now that her outraged college would recommend that her Fulbright scholarship be taken away, in which case she would have to leave Cambridge and come away without a degree, and please *what* was she to do?

I was a little taken aback, I remember, by the intensity of her fear and agitation, and, even more perhaps, by what I sensed to be a strong suppressed resentment: presumably, at Cambridge rules and practices, Cambridge dons and their demands, the Cambridge set-up as a whole perhaps. It was the first and the only time I glimpsed in Sylvia (without, of course, at the time knowing it for what it was) a small touch of the passionate *rage* which has since come to be recognized as a dominating emotion of her poetry, especially her last poems.

The problem of the illicit marriage was soon re
mollify her resentment, I said some soothing things a_
idiocy of Cambridge rules, and that the only way to live with
them was not to take their idiocy too much to heart. I suggested that she go to her tutor, make a full confession of her
crime, express a decent (though not abject) regret about not
having asked permission, and plead love, passion, the marriage of true minds, and so on, as the irresistible cause. She
was not however (I urged) to "criticize" the immortal rules or
moralize about their iniquity. I knew her tutor to be a warm-
hearted, rather romantic person, who I felt was likely to take a
kindly view of Sylvia's lapse. And so in the event it turned out.
Within a day or two Sylvia came back, happy and beaming.
Her tutor had been completely charming, kind, understanding; she would not have her Fulbright award taken away; and
she could now go and live with her legally recognized husband in any convenient place in Cambridge.

Soon after this, she and Ted moved into a small flat in
Eltisley Avenue, just round the corner from my own place in
Grantchester Meadows. She was passionately, brilliantly, happy:
incandescent with happiness, as Wendy Campbell has beautifully said. She spoke about it from time to time; and I remember at least once experiencing a thrill of fear at the idyllic
pitch and intensity of her happiness. What would happen (I
said, or half-said, to myself) if something should ever *go wrong*
with this marriage of true minds? Nothing of course would,
nothing *could*, go wrong: I was sublimely sure of this. Yet if,
inconceivably, it should, she would suffer terribly; I held my
breath to think how she would suffer. That was as far as my
momentary fear carried my imagination; nor was it possible it
should go further, in the face of her serenity, her tranquillity,
her confidence, and (most of all) her marvelous vitality, which
seemed a guarantee of limitless powers of resistance.

Sylvia mentioned during that winter that the flat in Eltisley
Avenue was bitterly cold. She hated cold, she said; it reduced

and diminished her, made her feel humiliated, degraded. I had a Fyrside oil-heater to spare, and offered to lend it to her for the winter. She accepted it with a gratitude quite in excess of the service, though obviously not of her need; and throughout the winter she kept on mentioning it, saying what a difference it made to their lives. I remembered the Fyrside (I should never have done so otherwise) when I read Alvarez's description of the icy London flat in which she killed herself. It tore at my heart to think how her anguish of spirit in those last months of her life must have been cruelly, intolerably, exacerbated by the cold she hated. . . .

During the time she and Ted were in America she wrote to me a few times. I came on a brief visit to America in the autumn of 1957, and stayed more than a fortnight [fourteen days] with relations in Cambridge, Mass. I tried to get in touch with her, in the hope that we could meet. But my letters were slow in reaching her, and in the end we only succeeded in having one telephone talk, on a very bad line. She was excited and moved, and so was I. I can't remember anything we said; I only remember it was the last time I heard her voice.

Presently she wrote to tell me that she and Ted were coming back to England. I remember the gist of that letter exactly: teaching at Smith was fine (she didn't say what has since become known, that she had taught brilliantly during that year); but it was a deadly distraction from writing, and she felt she must give it up, now or never, if she was to continue writing poetry. Ted felt the same, she said; and as he was not altogether happy in America, though he had made heroic efforts to acclimatize, they had decided to come back to England. I don't remember whether I wrote to her saying how much I applauded and blessed her decision, or just thought these things and never wrote. . . .

Plath Felt a Bitter Betrayal

The year (1959) in which Sylvia and Ted came back to England happened to be the year in which I was preparing to leave England, to settle in Israel. For reasons connected with this momentous decision (none of which seemed good enough afterward), I did not get in touch with them; and I left for Israel at the end of 1960 without having seen Sylvia again.

When three years later in Jerusalem I read of her death in the *Observer* notice, my horror, grief, incredulity, were the same as Wendy Campbell's. I didn't, however, even for one wild moment, fancy she had been murdered, as Wendy says she did. I could imagine only one possible cause. Something *had* after all gone wrong with the idyllic marriage of true minds. She had been, or felt herself to have been, now as never before, betrayed and abandoned; her anguish of loss, outraged pride, fury, resentment, despair—all mixed up, in what proportions one would never know—had unhinged her mind, and in her madness she had killed herself. I still knew nothing about *The Bell Jar*; and when a little later I learnt that my intuition about the marriage had been approximately correct, I felt her own kind of passionate, bitter rage: against the beautiful, impossible illusion itself, against the shattering, and the shatterer, of the illusion. I couldn't bring myself to write to Ted; I only heard in my head, over and over again, like a drum-beat, Othello's piercing words:

> But there, where I have garner'd up my heart,
>
> Where either I must live or bear no life,
>
> The fountain from the which my current runs
>
> Or else dries up; to be discarded thence!
>
> Or keep it as a cistern for foul toads
>
> To knot and gender in . . .

To be discarded thence, discarded, discarded; I seemed to see the word burning her heart to ashes in her last days in the freezing London flat. . . .

I have written these notes with much hesitation, feeling that I didn't have enough to say to justify the cost in the violation of privacy, or in relived anguish for myself. I feel I didn't know Sylvia in the least as well as other people knew her: Ted, or Wendy, or Alvarez, or almost any of the friends and admirers who have written about her. I didn't know *The Bell Jar* side of her at all; I didn't dream there was a part of her that was a kind of Catherine of [Emily Brontë's] *Wuthering Heights*, fighting (paradoxically, absurdly, for a Catherine nature) a hopeless battle to be an English don, a poet, a wife, a mother, and a charming woman all in one. I only knew her, really, as a beautiful, sensitive mind, ardently enjoying the exhilarations of the life of the intellect, living intensely, joyously, in the calm sunshine of the mind, as [philosopher David] Hume calls it. I saw her only, or almost only, in the radiance of this light, and what I saw was I think a real, inextinguishable part of her, though not the whole of her.

Sylvia Plath's Depression Was Inherited

Jane Feinmann

Jane Feinmann is a medical journalist and author of four books, including How to Have a Good Death.

Sylvia Plath's suicide became a literary event that sparked considerable controversy, according to Feinmann in the following viewpoint. Some critics blame Plath's husband, Ted Hughes, who deserted her for another woman, for her death. Her friend A. Alvarez claimed that Plath didn't really intend to commit suicide and instead was crying out for help. The truth behind her suicide was revealed by her doctor, John Horder, Feinmann maintains. Horder believed that Plath had an inherited tendency toward depression and pointed to the fact that Plath's paternal grandmother, aunt, and cousin also suffered from severe depression.

Thirty years after the American poet Sylvia Plath killed herself in London, the literary row over why she died is still going on. While some feminists claim that Plath was the victim of an insensitive husband, she is also accused of trying to manipulate the world around her once too often. But the doctor who cared for her in the last weeks of her life claims that the debate overlooks the real villian, and the subject of most of her poems and diary—the depression that dogged her life.

Plath's Suicide as Feminist Symbol

Plath's death on February 11, 1963, less than five months after she had separated from Ted Hughes, the present poet laureate [of the United Kingdom, until his death in 1998], made no

Jane Feinmann, "Rhyme, Reason and Depression," *Guardian*, February 16, 1993. Copyright © 1993 by Guardian News & Media Ltd. All rights reserved. Reproduced by permission.

more than a couple of paragraphs in the local paper and a few obituaries in the literary press. Soon, however, her death was attracting almost the same kind of ghoulish coverage as that of Marilyn Monroe, who died the previous year. After the posthumous publication of a collection of later poems in 1966, the international press discovered that the beautiful young American had written haunting works of genius about death and disillusionment before putting her head in the gas oven. Both *Time*, and *Life* magazines reviewed the slim volume, describing the 'strange and terrible' poems with a style 'as brutal as a truncheon' written during her 'last sick slide towards suicide'.

Plath's became a symbol of blighted female genius for the early feminist movement. She had chiselled out a literary career while doing her duty as wife and mother, and been rewarded by being abandoned with two children, no money and no proper home. American radical feminists openly accused Hughes of murder. In a 'holy war' In the seventies and early eighties, they harassed him during poetry readings, threatening to kill him. Plath's gravestone in Yorkshire was repeatedly defaced [by attempts to remove the "Hughes" from her name].

A different explanation came from the poet Al Alvarez in *The Savage God*, his 1971 book on suicide. He claimed that Hughes's view was that Plath had gambled with her death and that her suicide was an unanswered cry for help. Meanwhile, sympathisers of Hughes were claiming that she was a self-dramatising neurotic who had driven away a loving husband and then tried to force him back with a blackmailing suicide attempt. In a memoir in 1989, a neighbour recalled a woman with a 'morbidly prickly ego' who 'manipulated with the deep instinctive cunning of someone driven to get her way.'

Plath's Depression Was Inherited

Three months before her death, Plath had moved with her two small children into a flat near Dr John Horder, a GP [general practitioner] in Primrose Hill, North London. Now [in 1993] in his seventies, Horder is a former president of the Royal College of General Practitioners. A musician and painter himself, he was close to Plath just before her death. At a time when doctors labelled depression as neurosis, hypochondriasis and hysteria, he knew from experience the sheer physical pain of a severe depressive episode, made worse by shame and the conviction that life cannot improve.

Horder was also already aware that severe depression is triggered by much the same kind of stressful events and/or relationships that bring about normal depression. It is the over-reaction that marks out the illness. During her last depression, Plath had many reasons for feeling down. She had a virus infection and was looking after two young children on her own in a new flat during a particularly cold winter, while her husband had made another relationship. Yet all this was not in itself sufficient to push her to suicidal depression, Horder believes.

Every now and then, 'the neutral and impersonal forces of the world turn and come together in a thundercrack of judgment,' she wrote in her diary when she had slid into a depression after being the target of schoolboys' snowballs. 'There is no reason for the sudden terror, the feeling of condemnation, except that circumstances all mirror the inner doubt, the inner fear.'

The reason for 'the sudden terror', [Horder] believes, was that like himself, Plath had inherited a chemical imbalance that cause some kinds of depression just as an imbalance of insulin causes diabetes.

This physical and usually inherited background is by no means the cause of all depression. But it is relatively common, Horder believes—and moreover, the kind of depression that responds most effectively to medication.

As a young doctor Horder had been a Jungian [an adherent of Swiss psychologist Carl Jung] highly suspicious of the immorality of chemically interfering with the mind'. But circumstances converted him to the new anti-depressants launched in the late fifties. With a strong history of depression in his own family, he derived 'enormous comfort' from the recognition that the 'physical pain which gnawed at my life' was inherited, not his fault.

He has always been convinced that Plath had a similar family background. New research bears this out. Plath's father had died when she was 10, but his mother, sister and niece all suffered severe depression.

A few days before Plath's death, Horder prescribed her antidepressants. She was responding well, apparently understanding her struggle against the suicidal depression and reporting faithfully any side effects. But response to such drugs takes from ten to 20 days. At the time of her death, Horder says, she had reached the dangerous time when someone with suicidal tendencies is sufficiently roused from disabling lethargy to do something about it.

Knowing she was at risk alone with two young children he was visiting her daily and making strenuous efforts to have her admitted to hospital. When that failed, he arranged for a live-in nurse. She arrived five hours after Plath had opened the window of the children's bedroom, Sellotaped up the kitchen door, and placed her head on a small cloth inside the gas oven.

As she entered the house, the nurse found a note on the hall table saying: 'Phone Dr Horder' with his telephone number. Does that not suggest that she was expecting, somehow, to be rescued? Not at all, says Horder, who has repeatedly explained to biographers that she could not have been fooling around. 'No-one who saw the care with which the kitchen was prepared could have interpreted her action as anything but an irrational compulsion,' he says. His examination of her body at 10:30 am convinced him that she turned on the taps around 4 am, the time when the human metabolism is lowest and suicide is most common.

Plath's Death Could Have Been Prevented

Though her depression was inevitable, her death wasn't. He recalls feeling paralysed for weeks after the death and still wonders whether he could have done more to prevent it. He never read her poetry and did not know of the suicidal subject matter until long after, and is not certain that it would have made any difference if he had.

Certainly her life could have been managed more smoothly. She would not have been alone if her marriage had not come apart. But Horder says that blaming Hughes for her death makes no more sense than blaming Plath. Depression is a condition which affects not just the sufferer but everyone with whom they are in close contact, he says. . . .

No-one should underestimate the task of persuading people that depression is often an illness which needs to be treated with anti-depressants as well as by more fashionable psychological means. At present, ignorance is the root cause of many suicides, according to the Royal College of Psychiatrists. It is possible that Plath would still be alive today if she had consulted Horder earlier and started taking anti-depressants sooner.

Horder will not be drawn into such painful speculation. 'There are too many imponderables,' he says. No-one, however, would dispute that general understanding about depression has increased immeasurably since Sylvia Plath's death.

Social Issues
in Literature

CHAPTER 2

The Bell Jar and Depression

Sylvia Plath's Retelling of Her Mental Breakdown Lacks Power and Emotion

Saul Maloff

Saul Maloff is a literary critic and author of the novels Happy Families *and* Heartland.

The Bell Jar *is more autobiography than fiction, claims Maloff in the following viewpoint. Sylvia Plath's motivation in writing* The Bell Jar *was vengeful—she wanted to express her despair at losing her father and to vilify her mother, Maloff suggests. The novel itself has charm and wit, but no depth or passion, he contends, and it only hints at the powerful imagination of her later poetry.*

Apparent reasons for the eight-year delay in importing *The Bell Jar* from England (publication there, 1963) are not in themselves convincing. The pseudonym of Victoria Lucas was a hedge, but against what? Sylvia Plath made no secret of her authorship. Her suicide followed publication by a month, but such things have never stopped the wheels of industry from turning: she was a "property" after all, certainly following the publication of *Ariel* in 1966. Nor can we take seriously her having referred to it as a "potboiler" and therefore to be kept separate from her serious work: the oldest and most transparent of all writers' dodges. All the evidence argues against it: as early as 1957 she had written a draft of the novel; she completed the final version on a Eugene Saxton Fund fellowship and felt toward its terms an urgent sense of commitment and obligation; the painstaking quality of the writing—but above

Saul Maloff, "Waiting for the Voice to Crack," *The New Republic*, vol. 164, May 8, 1971, pp. 33–35. Copyright © 1971 by The New Republic, Inc. All rights reserved. Reproduced by permission of The New Republic.

all, its subject: her own pain and sickness, treated with literal fidelity, a journal done up as a novel, manifestly re-experienced, and not from any great distance of glowing health. One of her motives was the familiar one of getting her own back, to (as her heroine says) "fix a lot of people"— among others of smaller significance, to lay the ghost of her father, and tell the world she hated her mother (the exact words of her protagonist-surrogate, spoken to her psychiatrist in a key passage).

Mother Opposed *The Bell Jar*'s Publication

Only the names were changed, nothing else: as much as a novel can be, it was recorded rather than imagined. Evidently she panicked as publication drew near and displayed more than the usual terror of reviewers, who were on the whole generous and patronizing in a chuckling avuncular way, though she mis-read their intention, as toward the end, one supposes, she mis-read everything. Her last awful year was marked by a miscarriage, an appendectomy, the birth of her second child, as well as a series of plaguing minor illnesses, to say nothing of separation from her husband. According to her mother, Mrs. Aurelia Plath, whose 1970 letter to her daughter's Harper & Row editor is included in a "Biographical Note" appended to the novel, Miss Plath told her brother that the book must in no circumstances be published in the U.S.

Mrs. Plath's letter is a noteworthy document, and an oddly touching one. She pleads her case by telling the editor she knows no pleas will help, though publication here will cause "suffering" in the lives of several persons whom Sylvia loved and who had "given freely of time, thought, affection, and in one case, financial help during those agonizing six months of breakdown in 1953." To them, the book as it stands in itself "represents the basest ingratitude." But, Mrs. Plath argues, her daughter didn't mean for the book to stand alone; she herself told her mother in 1962 that she'd merely "thrown together events from my own life, fictionalizing to add color," a "pot-boiler" to show "how isolated a person feels when he is suffering a breakdown . . . to picture my world and the people in it as seen through the distorting lens of a bell jar." Her second novel, she assured her mother, "will show that same world as seen through the eyes of health." Ingratitude was "not the basis of Sylvia's personality"; the second novel, presumably, would have been one long, ingratiating, fictionalized thank-you note to the world. Of course the publisher is right to publish; but since the persons who may be slightly scorched are still alive, why [wait] eight years?

The Bell Jar Is Deceptively Bland

The novel itself is no firebrand. It's a slight, charming, sometimes funny and mildly witty, at moments tolerably harrowing "first" novel, just the sort of clever book a Smith summa cum laude (which she was) might have written if she weren't given to literary airs. From the beginning our expectations of scandal and startling revelation are disappointed by a modesty of scale and ambition and a jaunty temperateness of tone. The voice is straight out of the 1950's: politely disenchanted, wholesome, yes, wholesome, but never cloying, immediately attractive, nicely confused by it all, incorrigibly truth-telling; in short, the kind of kid we liked then, the best product of our best schools. The hand of [J.D.] Salinger lay heavy on her.

But this is 1971 and we read her analyst, too wily to be deceived by that decent, smiling, well-scrubbed coed who so wants to be liked and admired. We look for the slips and wait for the voice to crack. We want the bad, the worst news; that's what we're here for, to be made happy by horror, not to be amused by girlish chatter. Our interests are clinical and prurient. A hard case, she confounds us. She never raises her voice. To control it, she stays very close to the line of her life in her twentieth year, telling rather than evoking the memorable events; more bemused than aghast. That year she came down to New York from Smith one summer month to work as an apprentice-editor for *Mademoiselle* (here *Ladies Day*) for its college issue, a reward for being a good, straight-A girl and promising young writer; and had exactly the prescribed kind of time, meeting people and going places, eating out and dressing up, shopping and sightseeing, and thinking maybe it was about time she got laid. The closest she came to it was sleeping chastely, quite dressed and untouched, beside an inscrutable UN simultaneous translator. Throughout, the tone is prevailingly unruffled, matter-of-fact, humorously woebegone.

Prevailingly, but not quite. What should have been exciting—she was a small-town girl living in NYC for the first time on her own—was dreary, trivial, flat. She was beginning to doubt herself, her talent, her prospects. Mysteriously, as if from another work, period of life, region of the mind, images and memories startlingly appear, and just as quickly vanish; colors and events we recognize from the late poems: darkness and blackness; the world perceived as misshapen and ominous; her father (the figure of her marvelous poem "Daddy") remembered with love and fury, the source of her last "pure" happiness at the age of nine before he perversely left her bereft one day by cruelly dying; foetuses and blood, fever and sickness, the obsession with purity and the grotesque burden of her body, of feeling itself. In the poems the pressure is terrific; she screams her pain, in a final effort to contain it; yet here it is duly noted, set down serially, linearly, as possibly interesting to those in the business of making connections, scrupulously recorded as in a printed clinical questionnaire by a straight-A girl in the habit of carefully completing forms. When she sees the dumb, staring "goggle-eyed head lines" monstrously proclaiming the execution of the Rosenbergs,[1] she "couldn't help wondering what it would be like, being burned alive all along the nerves" and concludes flatly, "I

1. American Communists Julius and Ethel Rosenberg were executed in the electric chair for treason in 1953. The issue was controversial and drew ongoing media attention and commentary.

thought it must be the worst thing in the world." A silent china-white telephone sits like a "death's head." Her home-town boy-friend, a medical student, takes her to see cadavers at the morgue and a foetus with a "little piggy smile" that re-minds her of [President Dwight D.] Eisenhower; and then, to round things off, they go to watch a child-birth. The woman on the "awful torture-table, with these metal stirrups sticking up in mid-air" seems to her "to have nothing but an enor-mous spider-fat stomach and two little ugly spindly legs propped in the high stirrups" and "all the time the baby was being born she never stopped making this unhuman wooing noise" and "all the time, in some secret part of her, that long, blind, doorless and windowless corridor of pain was waiting to open up and shut her in again." A silly, simpering girl, a hat-designer idiotically pleased at the good news of the Rosenbergs' execution, reveals a "dybbuk" [a malevolent ghost] beneath her plump, bland exterior. But these darker notes do not accumulate to thematic density save in retrospect; they seem accidental dissonances, slips of the tongue.

The Bell Jar Lacks Complexity

Even the breakdown, when it comes, is generally muted, seem-ing from the outside as much slothfulness as madness, the obligatory junior-year interlude. The break is quantitative: the tones are darker, the world somewhat more distorted and re-mote, the voice, almost over breezy now, is more than disaf-fected—it can become nasty, a trifle bitchy, even cruel, streaked with violence. She makes some gestures toward suicide—as much amusing as they are frightening; and then though she very nearly brings it off, we almost can't bring ourselves to be-lieve it, so theatrically staged is the scene. Yet even then, after breakdown and hospitalization, electroshock and insulin, she composes the book's funniest, most charming scene—of her incidental, much-delayed defloration [loss of virginity]; and in the knowledge of its appalling consequences. The chap, accidentally encountered on the steps of the Widener [Library at Harvard] (where else?) is, she carefully notes, a 26-year-old full professor of Mathematics at Harvard, name of Irwin; and ugly. Him she elects to "seduce"; and after the fastest such episode in fiction, she isn't even sure it happened at all. Wanting more direct evidence, she can only infer it from her massive hemorrhaging. Concluding now that, no longer a virgin, she has put behind her childish things, she lies down and, bleeding profusely, writes: "I smiled into the dark. I felt part of a great tradition." At the end, the tone is ambiguous but not despairing; she has been readmitted to Smith, where out of old habit she will keep getting nothing but A's; the bell jar has descended once, and may again.

She laid out the elements of her life, one after the other, and left to the late poems the necessary work of imagining and creating it: it is for this reason that we feel in the book an absence of weight and complexity sufficient to the subject.

On balance, *The Bell Jar*, good as it is, must be counted part of Sylvia Plath's juvenilia [immature works], along with most of the poems of her first volume; though in the novel as in a few of the early poems she foretells the last voice she was ever to command.

Plath Uses Literary Doubles to Depict the Anguish of Her Schizophrenia

Gordon Lameyer

Gordon Lameyer was a professor, writer, and editor who was romantically involved with Sylvia Plath from the time they met in college until Plath met and fell in love with Ted Hughes. Lameyer has written numerous articles about Plath.

Plath was profoundly influenced by the work of Fyodor Dostoevsky and his literary use of the double, contends Lameyer in the following viewpoint. She employed a similar technique in The Bell Jar, *populating the book with pairs who represent the conflicting aspects of the heroine's personality. Unfortunately, Plath failed to understand the root of her schizophrenia and was destroyed by it, rather than transforming it into literature, Lameyer argues.*

[The] place where Sylvia Plath explored the psychological double to the fullest was in her semiautobiographical novel, *The Bell Jar*.

Sylvia Plath's study of the double in two of Fyodor Dostoevsky's novels, as recorded by her as yet unpublished Smith College honor's thesis, *The Magic Mirror* (1955), provided her with insights for the structure of the doubles in her own novel. When she returned to Smith in the spring of 1954 to repeat the second half of her junior year, Sylvia became interested in Dostoevsky from a course on the Russian novel given by George Gibian, who became her senior honors' thesis advisor the following year. In dramatizing the projection of

Gordon Lameyer, "The Double in Sylvia Plath's *The Bell Jar*," in *Sylvia Plath: Method and Madness*, ed. Edward Butscher. Tuscon, AZ: Schaffner Press, 1976, pp. 143–65. Copyright © 1976 by Schaffner Press. All rights reserved. Reproduced by permission.

the schizophrenic's fears upon a double figure, Dostoevsky gave her a deeper understanding of her own nervous breakdown, attempted suicide, and recuperation than had her limited psychoanalysis at McLean, the mental hospital where she had spent four months.

Written in the fall of 1954, *The Magic Mirror* is a scholarly analysis of the dynamics of "the double," first, in Dostoevsky's early novella by that name about Golyadkin, a functionary who drives himself mad with the hallucination of his own projected double, and, second, in the great study of parricide, *The Brothers Karamazov*. In the latter, Ivan evolves two kinds of doubles. One is a hallucinatory figure, the Devil, and the other is his bastard brother, Smerdyakov. Perhaps the image of the bastard double suggested the final startling image for her later parricidal poem, "Daddy."

At the time of the writing of her thesis, Sylvia told me that she was terribly frustrated in not being able to understand German well enough to read the definitive study called *The Double* by the psychoanalyst Otto Rank. In the notes for her thesis she does refer to three of his articles, but unfortunately she did not read Rank's book. It was not until 1971 that an English translation was made of Rank's book by Harry Tucker, Jr., published by University of North Carolina Press. Had it been available, Rank's book would have provided her not only with additional background on the double in literature and anthropology but also with a vital insight, I think, into the connection between narcissism and the double. According to modern psychoanalytic theory, it is the narcissist's failure to fulfill love needs in childhood that causes the personality to split, projecting onto another the deepest guilts and destructive forces within the self. . . .

Plath Used Doubles in *The Bell Jar*

The Bell Jar is full of "doubles," mirror images that polarize the attitudes of the heroine toward herself and toward others.

Some of the "doubles" are positive and innocent, while others represent antipathies or the repressed, Iibidinal urges of the heroine. But the technique of structuring the conflict Sylvia derived from Dostoevsky. The analysis which she makes of the novella, *The Double*, in the first half of her thesis sheds light on the heroine Esther Greenwood all throughout her breakdown and the first part of her hospitalization. However, unlike Golyadkin, Esther does not go mad but rallies and gets well. In this sense she is like the heroine of the much more romantic *I Never Promised You a Rose Garden*, [by Joanne Greenberg], which, along with the writings of [Scots psychiatrist] R.D. Laing, has gone a long way toward uncovering the anguish of a schizophrenic; but not with the poetic intensity of Sylvia Plath.

As distilled in the second half of her thesis, what Sylvia learned from the kind of reconciliation achieved by Ivan Karamazov with himself through his understanding of his guilt and his acceptance of responsibility gave Sylvia an insight into her own conflicts that caused her to see the world unconsciously in doubles. *The Brothers Karamazov* provided a way— but a very different way—to resolve the heroine's incipient madness in *The Bell Jar*. By killing off her own primary double, Sylvia Plath rearranged her own experience so that at the end her heroine could be free of her bell jar of "stifling distortions" and become physically reborn. . . .

The Double Survives, Plath Does Not

The terrible irony of *The Bell Jar* is that the original of Joan Gilling, the double that Sylvia kills off so that Esther can live, is very much alive, and that it is Sylvia who has been successful in killing herself. Many critics have noted the irony that Sylvia prophetically sensed at the end of the novel that in Europe the bell jar might descend again. But it did not descend for her double. The girl whom Sylvia knew in Wellesley and at Smith College and whom she felt had followed her to McLean

The Russian author Fyodor Dostoevsky. Gordon Lameyer notes that Sylvia Plath was profoundly influenced by Dostoevsky, in particular his literary use of the double, a technique Plath employs in The Bell Jar. © Imagno/Getty Images.

is actually very unlike the Joan Gilling who has lesbian leanings toward another inmate. In fact, Sylvia very much admired and liked the original girl. Was Sylvia, then, projecting her deepest fears onto the double of her heroine? After all, Esther gets a perverse thrill at Joan's funeral as she becomes stronger, more able to face the bright, snow-filled world. Knowing both Sylvia and the original of Joan Gilling well at the time of the events depicted in the novel and for several years afterward, I can testify that neither girl had inclinations in this direction. I think we must seek the roots of Sylvia's disturbance in another psychological area.

Otto Rank says that when a narcissist experiences the loss of a double it sometimes demonstrates only his intense interest in himself:

> Thus the apparent contradiction—the loss of the shadow-image or mirror-image represented as pursuits understood as a representation of the opposite, the recurrence of what is repressed in that which represses. . . .

> This same mechanism is shown by the denouement of madness, almost regularly leading to suicide, which is so frequently linked with pursuit by the double, the self. Even when the depiction does not measure up to Dostoevsky's unsurpassable clinical exactitude, it does become clear that it is a question of paranoid ideas of pursuit and influencing to which the hero is prey by reason of his double. Since [Sigmund] Freud's psychoanalytic clarification of paranoia, we know that this illness has as a basis "a fixation in narcissism," to which corresponds typical megalomania, the sexual overrating of oneself. The stage of development from which paranoids regress to their original narcissism is sublimated homosexuality, against the undisguised eruption of which they defend themselves with the characteristic mechanism of projection. On the basis of this insight, it can easily be shown that the pursuit of the ill person regularly proceeds from the originally loved persons (or their surrogates).

Sylvia never loved the original of Joan Gilling, but she did greatly admire her at one time. For Esther, Joan finally represents all the puritanical ethos present in the world of Buddy and Mrs. Willard. She has to be rejected, much as was the extravagantly wild double, Doreen, rejected earlier. But why did Sylvia feel the necessity to alter her experience and kill off this particular double?

Otto Rank explains:

> The frequent slaying of the double, through which the hero seeks to protect himself permanently from the pursuits of his self, is really a suicidal act. It is, to be sure, in the painless form of slaying a different ego: an unconscious illusion of the splitting-off of a bad, culpable ego—a separation which, moreover, appears to be the precondition for every suicide. The suicidal person is unable to eliminate by direct self-destruction the fear of death resulting from the threat to his narcissism. To be sure, he seizes upon the only possible way out, suicide, but he is incapable of carrying it out other than by way of the phantom of a feared and hated double, because he loves and esteems his ego too highly to give it pain or to transform the idea of his destruction into the deed. In this subjective meaning, the double turns out to be a functional expression of the psychological fact that the individual with an attitude of this kind cannot free himself from a certain phase of his narcissistically loved ego-development.

Sylvia Misunderstood Her Schizophrenia

I have to conclude, then, that Sylvia was trying to free herself from certain negative attitudes she recognized within herself, puritanical attitudes which she associated with Mrs. Willard and which she projected in a perversion of sexual purity upon her double. Although Rank notes above that "the stage of development from which paranoids regress 'to their original narcissism is sublimated homosexuality," I do not think it applies to Sylvia. I knew her too well at the time of the incidents related in *The Bell Jar* ever to conclude that she had lesbian tendencies. Aside from the original of Buddy Willard, I am the only person, I believe, who has ever dated both Sylvia and the original of Joan Gilling. Although certainly neither girl was inclined toward lesbianism, Sylvia understood enough of the love-hate duality of rivals to suggest this characteristic in her artistic double.

I feel that it was Sylvia's narcissism, developing from the loss of love, beginning at the time of her father's death, that caused her to project upon innocent and evil doubles her conflicting polarized selves. As an artist, she fully understood this inner conflict and, with Dostoevsky's help, created a vehicle for its expression. Had Otto Rank's *The Double* been translated before 1963, Sylvia might have understood and accepted the etiological [causal] conclusion that her incipient schizophrenia stemmed from narcissism and might have transformed it, as she transformed so much of her experience, into art.

Illness Pervades *The Bell Jar*

Howard Moss

Howard Moss, an American poet, literary critic, and dramatist, was poetry editor of the New Yorker *for nearly forty years before his death in 1987.*

The Bell Jar *is disturbing because it describes madness and attempted suicide, but there is no evidence that Sylvia Plath understood either, Moss argues in the following viewpoint. Illness and pain are constant motifs in the book, at first described humorously. Even the heroine's descent into depression and madness is handled with detachment. Although the book ends optimistically, the reader is not convinced, Moss maintains.*

The story of a poet who tries to end her life written by a poet who did, Sylvia Plath's "The Bell Jar" was first published under a pseudonym in England in 1963, one month before she committed suicide. We have had to wait almost a decade for its publication in the United States, but it was reissued in England in 1966 under its author's real name. A biographical note in the present edition makes it plain that the events in the novel closely parallel Sylvia Plath's twentieth year. For reasons for which we are not wholly to blame, our approach to the novel is impure; "The Bell Jar" is fiction that cannot escape being read in part as autobiography. It begins in New York with an ominous lightness, grows darker as it moves to Massachusetts, then slips slowly into madness. Esther Greenwood, one of a dozen girls in and on the town for a month as "guest editors" of a teen-age fashion magazine, is the product of a German immigrant family and a New England suburb. With "fifteen years of straight A's" behind her, a depressing at-

Howard Moss, "Dying: An Introduction," *The New Yorker*, July 10, 1971, pp. 73–74.
Copyright © 1971 by the Estate of Howard Moss. All rights reserved. Reproduced by permission.

tachment to a dreary but handsome medical student, Buddy Willard, still unresolved, and a yearning to be a poet, she is the kind of girl who doesn't know what drink to order or how much to tip a taxi driver but is doing her thesis on the "twin images" in "Finnegans Wake" [by James Joyce], a book she has never managed to finish. Her imagination is at war with the small-town tenets of New England and the big-time sham of New York. She finds it impossible to be one of the army of college girls whose education is a forced stop on the short march to marriage. The crises of identity, sexuality, and survival are grim, and often funny. Wit, irony, and intelligence as well as an inexplicable, withdrawn sadness separate Esther from her companions. Being an involuntary truth-seeker, she uses irony as a weapon of judgment, and she is its chief victim. Unable to experience or mime emotions, she feels defective as a person. The gap between her and the world widens: "I couldn't get myself to react. I fell very still and very empty." . . . "The silence depressed me. It wasn't the silence of silence. It was my own silence." . . . "That morning I had tried to hang myself."

Sickness Is a Theme

Camouflage and illness go together in "The Bell Jar"; moreover, illness is often used to lift or tear down a façade. Doreen, a golden girl of certainty admired by Esther, begins the process by getting drunk. The glimpse of her lying with her head in a pool of her own vomit in a hotel hallway is repellent but crucial. Her illness is followed by a mass ptomaine poisoning at a "fashion" lunch. Buddy gets tuberculosis and goes off to a sanatorium. Esther, visiting him, breaks her leg skiing. When she has her first sexual experience, with a young math professor she has picked up, she hemorrhages. Taken in by a lesbian friend, she winds up in a hospital. Later, she learns that the friend has hanged herself. A plain recital of the events in "The Bell Jar" would be ludicrous if they were not balanced by genuine desperation at one side of the scale and a sure sense of black comedy at the other. Sickness and disclosure are the keys to "The Bell Jar." On her last night in New York, Esther climbs to the roof of her hotel and throws her city wardrobe over the parapet, piece by piece. By the end of the novel, she has tried to get rid of her very life, which is given back to her by another process of divestment—psychiatry. Pain and gore are endemic to "The Bell Jar," and they are described objectively, self-mockingly, almost humorously to begin with. Taken in by the tone (the first third of "The Bell Jar" might be a mordant, sick-joke version of "Breakfast at Tiffany's"), the reader is being lured into the lion's den—that sterile cement room in the basement of a mental hospital where the electric-shock-therapy machine waits for its frightened clients.

Esther Is Conflicted

The casualness with which physical suffering is treated suggests that Esther is cut off from the instinct for sympathy right from the beginning—for herself as well as for others. Though she is enormously aware of the impingements of sensation, her sensations remain impingements. She lives close to the nerve, but the nerve has become detached from the general network. A thin layer of glass separates her from everyone, and the novel's title, itself made of glass, is evolved from her notion of disconnection: the head of each mentally ill person is enclosed in a bell jar, choking on his own foul air.

Torn between conflicting roles—the sweetheart-*Hausfrau*—mother and "the life of the poet," neither very real to her—Esther finds life itself inimical. Afraid of distorting the person she is yet to become, she becomes the ultimate distortion—nothing. As she descends into the pit of depression, the world is a series of wrong reverberations: her mother's face is a perpetual accusation, the wheeling of a baby carriage underneath her window a grinding irritation. She becomes obsessed by the idea of suicide, and one of the great achievements of

In The Bell Jar, *Esther Greenwood likens her depression to being trapped in a bell jar.* © Bill Binzen/Corbis.

"The Bell Jar" is that it makes real the subtle distinctions between a distorted viewpoint and the distortions inherent in what it sees. Convention may contribute to Esther's insanity, but she never loses her awareness of the irrationality of convention. Moved to Belsize, a part of the mental hospital reserved for patients about to go back to the world, she makes the connection explicit:

> What was there about us, in Belsize, so different from the girls playing bridge and gossiping and studying in the college to which I would return? Those girls, too, sat under bell jars of a sort.

Terms like "mad" and "sane" grow increasingly inadequate as the action develops. Esther is "psychotic" by definition, but the definition is merely a descriptive tag; by the time we learn how she got to be "psychotic" the word has ceased to be relevant. (As a work of fiction, "The Bell Jar" seems to complement the clinical theories of the Scottish analyst R.D. Laing.) Because it is written from the distraught observer's point of view rather than from the viewpoint of someone observing her, there is continuity to her madness; it is not one state suddenly supplanting another but the most gradual of processes.

Suicide, a grimly compulsive game of fear and guilt, as addictive as alcohol or drugs, is experimental at first—a little blood here, a bit of choking there, just to see what it will be like. It quickly grows into an overwhelming desire for annihilation. By the time Esther climbs into the crawl space of a cellar and swallows a bottle of sleeping pills—by the time we are faced by the real thing—the event, instead of seeming grotesque, seems like a natural consequence. When she is about to leave the hospital, after a long series of treatments, her psychiatrist tells her to consider her breakdown "a bad dream." Esther, "patched, retreaded, and approved for the road," thinks, "To the person in the bell jar, blank and stopped as a dead baby, the word itself is the bad dream."

A Choice Between Life or Death

That baby is only one of many in "The Bell Jar." They smile up from the pages of magazines, they sit like little freaks pickled in glass jars on display in the pediatric ward of Buddy's hospital. A "sweet baby cradled in its mother's belly" seems to wait for Esther at the end of the ski run when she has her accident. And in the course of the novel she witnesses a birth. In place of her never-to-be-finished thesis on the "twin images," in "Finnegans Wake," one might be written on the number and kinds of babies that crop up in "The Bell Jar." In a gynecologist's office, watching a mother fondling her baby, Esther wonders why she is so separated from this easy happiness, this carrying out of the prescribed biological and social roles. She does not want a baby; she is a baby herself. But she is also a potential writer. She wants to fulfill herself, not to *be* fulfilled. To her, babies are The Trap, and sex is the bait. But she is too intelligent not to realize that babies don't represent life, they *are* life, though not necessarily the kind Esther wants to live; that is, if she wants to live at all. She is caught between the monstrous fetuses on display in Buddy's ward and the monstrous slavery of the seemingly permanent pregnancy of her neighbor Dodo Conway, who constantly wheels a baby carriage under Esther's window, like a demented figure in a Greek chorus. Babies lure Esther toward suicide by luring her toward a life she cannot—literally—bear. There seem to be only two solutions, and both involve the invisible: to pledge faith to the unborn or fealty to the dead. Life, so painfully visible and present, defeats her, and she takes it, finally, into her own hands. With the exception of the psychiatrist's disinterested affection for her, love is either missing or unrecognized in "The Bell Jar." Its overwhelming emotion is disgust—disgust that has not yet become contempt and is therefore more damaging. . . .

"The Bell Jar" lacks the coruscating magnificence of the late poems. Something girlish in its manner betrays the hand of the amateur novelist. Its material, after all, is what has been transcended. It is a frightening book, and if it ends on too optimistic a note as both fiction and postdated fact, its real terror lies elsewhere. Though we share every shade of feeling that leads to Esther's attempts at suicide, there is not the slightest insight in "The Bell Jar" into suicide itself. That may be why it bears the stamp of authority. Reading it, we are up against the raw experience of nightmare, not the analysis or understanding of it.

The Ending of *The Bell Jar* Is Cautiously Optimistic

Caroline King Barnard

A literary critic, Caroline King Barnard is the author of a biography of poet Anne Sexton.

In The Bell Jar *Sylvia Plath's alter ego Esther Greenwood has two best friends who represent different aspects of her divided personality, according to Barnard in the following viewpoint. Betsy is naïve and pure, and Doreen is worldly and sexy. Following her suicide attempt and treatment, Esther casts off role playing and accepts herself as she really is, Barnard writes. The novel ends on an optimistic note, with Esther fully recovered, married, and a mother, the critic concludes, but there is a warning suggested by the analogy to a retreaded tire, however, as retreads are weaker than new tires.*

The subject of Sylvia Plath's English honors thesis, on which she worked after returning to college in 1954, was the literary treatment of the double. In *The Bell Jar*, Plath not only creates a similar scholarly interest for Esther Greenwood; she also provides fictional realization of the device. Elly Higginbottom is Esther Greenwood's other self, the embodiment of her fantasy. Esther's dilemma, her "split personality" as she calls it, is dramatized in the novel's opening chapter by her inability to decide between two potential "best friends." Vacillating between the innocent, wholesome Betsy and the urbane, sexy Doreen, she finds herself unable to form a complete identification with either one, since she herself is divided, in a similar way, between conditioning and desire. To express that inner division, Esther Greenwood creates Elly Higginbottom. . . .

Caroline King Barnard, "The Bell Jar," in *Sylvia Plath*. Belmont, CA: Gale, 1978, pp. 24–33. www.cengage.com/permissions. Copyright © 1978 by Gale, a part of Cengage Learning, Inc. All rights reserved. Reproduced by permission.

Esther Borrows the Identity of Others

It is appropriate for Elly to have neither family nor roots, for she represents escape from all of the pressures which are the source of Esther's present confusion. In so doing, she brings that confusion into sharper relief. Esther is an unwilling captive of her background and conditioning; external familial and social pressures war with her natural instincts, and her level of self-confidence is far too low for those instincts to assert themselves sufficiently. Her naive expectations of sex and marriage, for example, have been thoroughly conditioned by her mother and by others: to be acceptable as a wife she must remain a virgin, and after marriage she must assume a submissive domestic role. Instinctively she rebels against these notions, partly because she naturally senses their limitations, and partly because she discovers that men are not bound by similar premarital rules. The confusion thereby produced is extreme. For nineteen-year-old Esther, "pureness [is] the great issue." Because she does not want "infinite security and to be the place an arrow shoots off from," as advocated by Buddy Willard and his mother, she decides that she must never marry. And because she now sees "the world divided into people who had slept with somebody and people who hadn't," she resolves to cross "the boundary line." Yet her conditioning remains a powerful influence; she can be comfortable with neither alternative.

Indeed, Esther finds it impossible to pursue either alternative in even a remotely satisfying way. "I wondered," she muses, "why I couldn't go the whole way doing what I should any more. This made me sad and tired. Then I wondered why I couldn't go the whole way doing what I shouldn't, . . . and this made me even sadder and more tired." This is the tiredness of depression which Esther feels, a depression produced by the immobility which baffles and frustrates her. Esther is indeed trapped within the stifling confines of the bell jar.

Unable to establish and nurture a self-identity which will afford her some measure of security, Esther is reduced to deriving her identity from the expectations of others. She acts. For Doreen, she must be worldly and blasé; for Buddy Willard, she must be pure and virginal; for Jay Cee, she must be intelligent and ambitious; for Mrs. Willard, she must be domestic and submissive. For her mother, she must be the good daughter, appropriately grateful, successful, and innocent. And above all, she must maintain at any cost a proper appearance of health and sanity, not, as her mother puts it, "like that," like "those awful dead people at that hospital." The more Esther acts in these ways, the more she loses touch with her self. The result is further loss of confidence and growing disorientation.

Another result of her role-playing is that Esther feels placed in an increasingly defensive position, for in responding to the expectations of others, she allows herself to be constantly acted upon. She comes, therefore, to see her environment as increasingly hostile and threatening. Things accost her. On a skiing trip with Buddy, the rope tow is a "rough, bruising snake of a rope that slithered through [my fingers]." People menace her. Elly-Esther is terrified by the "brown figure in sensible flat brown shoes" whose appearance on the Boston Common abruptly ends her conversation with the sailor; in the presence of this ominous Mrs. Willard–Mrs. Greenwood person, Esther feels stricken with fear and guilt about her present behavior. She also experiences a sudden, sharp insight: "I thought what an awful woman that lady in the brown suit had been, and how she . . . was responsible for my taking the wrong turn here and the wrong path there and for everything bad that happened after that." Men especially threaten her; their reality always fails her expectation. The woman-hating Marco actually attacks her. From her experience with Buddy Willard, she knows that as "flawless" as men may seem "off in the distance," they would not "do at all" when they "moved closer." Marriage, then, is impossible for Esther, since she knows that any man, even the handsome Constantin, would require that his wife become a domestic drudge, like Mrs. Willard's kitchen mat. Sex terrifies her; Esther's description of Buddy's penis is particularly devastating and dehumanizing: "The only thing I could think of was turkey neck and turkey gizzards."

Esther Feels Powerless and Victimized

It is this frame of mind which the novel's [Julius and Ethel] Rosenberg motif illuminates. The summer Esther Greenwood goes to New York is also, as *The Bell Jar*'s opening lines reveal, "the summer they electrocuted the Rosenbergs" [for treason]. Esther observes: "It had nothing to do with me, but I couldn't help wondering what it would be like, being burned alive all along your nerves." Despite the disclaimer, the Rosenbergs' experience comes to have a great deal to do with Esther. By the time she becomes Dr. Gordon's patient, her confusion is far advanced; virtually incapable of action, she has become the helpless object of the acts of others. The clumsily applied shock treatment represents the epitome of such acts, and significantly, it comes to serve as the symbol of Esther's paranoia and the total collapse of her perspective. The Rosenbergs, possibly innocent, but helpless before the judgment of their accusers, have been put to death by electrocution. Esther instinctively equates their experience with her own; like the Rosenbergs, she feels powerless and victimized, threatened and judged by everyone and everything. Thus, as her own experience with electric shock commences, Esther wonders "what terrible thing it was that I had done."

Esther Withdraws to Escape Reality

Placed in such a precarious emotional position by her insecurity and disorientation, the embattled Esther finds it more and more difficult to connect inner with outer reality. She is caught in a vicious round of destructive activity, for, as her behavior has indicated, her very efforts at coping with her world also reinforce her isolation. Her voice expresses the dilemma. Esther's tone, especially up to the time of her recovery under Dr. Nolan's guidance, is similar to the tone of such late poems as "Lady Lazarus" and "The Applicant": carefully postured, mocking, caustic, defensively nonchalant. It is the voice which Esther feels encouraged by Doreen's influence to develop: "wise and cynical as all hell." Esther's wit is brilliant, and her humorous observations are incisive. Such a voice can protect, but it can also protect too well, building an impregnable barrier between its speaker and the world, between the self and other people.

This condition is realized in the novel's dominant image; Esther feels as though she is "being stuffed farther and farther into a black, airless sack with no way out." She is increasingly unable to deal with her environment, progressively helpless to "steer anything, not even myself," powerless to "get myself to react." The glass walls of the bell jar permit only a tantalizing, often distorted visual contact between inside and outside; all other forms of mutual communication are impossible. And the interior environment not only isolates; it stifles. Esther observes: "The air of the bell jar wadded round me and I couldn't stir."

Total withdrawal becomes Esther's only course of action. "To the person in the bell jar ... the world itself is the bad dream," she concludes, and escape from that present dream with its impossible demands and pressures can be achieved only by return to an earlier, simpler time. "I was only purely happy," she observes, "until I was nine years old": what she seeks, then, is the singleness, the simplicity, and the purity of infancy.

The actions which Esther takes to achieve this end involve a kind of ritual purgation, a means by which she can free herself of uncleanliness or confusion or guilt. To restore herself to a state of simple purity, she must destroy or dissolve all evidence of the present "bad dream." It is this kind of action which Sylvia Plath employs also in the imagery of many of her last poems; release from the oppression of the speaker's present condition is often expressed in terms of death, purification, and rebirth. Similarly, Esther Greenwood, having returned from an evening of being Elly with Doreen and Lenny, seeks to rid herself of the whole dirty, oppressive experience through the rebirth of a sort of baptism. . . .

The bath, in this case, achieves the required retrogression, restoring Esther's spirit without doing violence to her body. As her sense of oppression intensifies, however, so does her need for escape, rendering her ever more careless of physical consequences. Buddy Willard's proposal of marriage places Esther in a particularly critical position, especially since her refusal expresses a rebellion she is not equipped to handle. Skiing with Buddy shortly thereafter, then, she again seeks to rid herself of her present world with its intolerable pressures and demands; this time her need is so great that even the death of her physical body is of no consequence: "the thought that I might kill myself formed in my mind coolly as a tree or a flower." An inexperienced skier, she takes off down the hill: "I thought, 'this is what it is to be happy.' I plummeted down past the zigzaggers, the students, the experts, through year after year of doubleness and smiles and compromise, into my own past. People and trees receded on either hand like the dark sides of a tunnel as I hurtled on to the still, bright point at the end of it, the pebble at the bottom of the well, the white sweet baby cradled in its mother's belly."

From here, there is only a small step to Esther's actual suicide attempt, for that act represents for her a total withdrawal to the "pure" and "sweet" condition of infancy. The location she chooses is a dark hole beneath her house, a "secret, earth-bottomed crevice" leading from the cellar, which is lit only by "a dim, undersea light." After some effort, Esther crawls into the hole, "crouch[ing] at the mouth of the darkness," and cov-

Caroline King Barnard points out that although The Bell Jar *ends optimistically, the metaphor of a retreaded tire serves as a warning: just as retreads are more likely than new tires to fall apart, Esther's recovery may not last.* © Car Culture/Corbis.

ers the entrance with a log. The earth inside her womb-like retreat is "friendly"; the dark feels "thick as velvet"; the cobwebs are soft; she curls up and takes her sleeping pills.

Esther Undergoes a Rebirth

From this experience, Esther does achieve a sort of rebirth, though perhaps not precisely the variety she had expected. Her suicide attempt fails, and she is hospitalized. Yet, in her total collapse, she has reached a kind of infancy, from which she can grow. Depressed beyond the point of caring about "the doubleness and smiles and compromise," and encouraged by the sensitive Dr. Nolan to rediscover herself on her own terms, Esther slowly constructs for herself a new and better-integrated personality.

She learns to free herself from the tyranny of others' expectations. Helpless to act even defensively during the days immediately following her suicide attempt, she has no choice but to appear exactly as she is. Her legs may look "disgusting and ugly" when Buddy Willard comes to visit, but she makes no move to hide them. "'That's me,'" she thinks. "'That's what I am'." When a group of medical students passing her bed greet her with the customary "How are you feeling?" she responds not with the expected "Fine" but with a truthful "I feel lousy." Once she is able to reveal her true self in this rudimentary way, Esther develops new confidence and perspective. In the presence of her hospital visitors, she identifies the tyranny which has held her captive, and she grows to hate these visits, since she knows that the visitors measure her, "fat and stringy hair against what I had been and what they wanted me to be." She now sees that such an attitude has motivated even the apparently beneficent interest of people like Jay Cee and the famous career-oriented woman poet at her college: "they all wanted to adopt me in some way, and, for the price of their care and influence, have me resemble them." Slowly Esther grows to understand the futility of building her identity on the expectations of people like these.

Perhaps the visitor most threatening to Esther's new perspective is her mother. Of all the forces which have kept Esther divided against herself, her mother has been the most powerful, looming up as she did that day on the Boston Common to assert her influence. Pious self-abnegation has been one of the mother's tools, and she attempts to use it still; during one of her visits, "my mother told me I should be grateful. She said I had used up almost all her money." Guilt keeps the daughter under control, and Esther, while seeing herself manipulated in this way, nevertheless feels the bell jar descending around her once again. On other occasions, however, Esther challenges her mother's influence more successfully. Of all her visitors, Esther observes, "my mother was the worst. She never scolded me, but kept begging me, with a sorrowful face, to tell her what she had done wrong." Following one of these sessions she dares to reveal to Dr. Nolan that she hates her mother—and then waits "for the blow to fall." Marvelously, however, Dr. Nolan replies only that "'I suppose you do.'" With such support, Esther grows able to accept and deal with her rebellion. She recalls a recent visit from her mother, her face "a pale, reproachful moon." "A daughter in an asylum! I had done that to her" had been the mother's implied message. And "with her sweet, martyr's smile," she had said: "'We'll take up where we left off, Esther.... We'll act as if this were a bad dream.'" But Esther now knows that she must do nothing of the kind.

Indeed, Esther achieves sufficient perspective to see that her struggle against the tyranny of custom and expectation is not hers alone, but is generally characteristic of the human condition. Her hospital environment is little different from the college environment which she has left and to which she will return. Like her and her hospital friends, her college friends, "too, sat under bell jars of a sort." Further, her new perspective allows her to deal with the "bad dream" from which her mother wishes her to seek escape. "Remember[ing] everything," she can now shun the idea that "forgetfulness, like a kind of snow, should numb and cover" the particulars of that nightmare. For "they were part of me. They were my landscape." The bell jar has been raised; it now hangs, "suspended, a few feet above my head. I was open to the circulating air."

Esther Finds New Freedom

Several other events herald Esther's emergence from the stifling confines of the bell jar. For the first time since the opening of her narrative, she laughs. In a conversation with Buddy Willard concerning the suicide of their friend Joan, Esther, confident in her own evaluation of the situation and accurate in her assessment of Buddy's confusion, "burst out laughing." To be sure, Esther's observations throughout the course of her narrative have not been without humor, but this laugh is different. This is not, like the others, an inward-directed, self-conscious quip or a sardonic gibe; it is the outward-directed, spontaneous response of a person secure enough to have no need of sarcasm. And that laugh, as it signals Esther's new freedom from the tyranny of her old self, provides a new perspective for the reader as well; the barriers between Esther and the world are removed not only for Esther, but also for her audience.

Joan's death affords Esther another opportunity to exercise her new perspective. During the conversation in which Esther laughs, Buddy is concerned that he, somehow, is responsible for the suicide attempts of Joan and Esther, both of whom he had dated. Esther, having already overcome, with Dr. Nolan's help, the fear of her own culpability, now assumes the role of healer as she allays Buddy's apprehensions. Even more important for Esther, however, is the symbolic significance of Joan's death. "I wondered," she muses at Joan's funeral, "what I thought I was burying." Like the old Esther, Joan has been tyrannized by the brown Boston Common mother figure, yet Joan has been unable to identify the source of her oppression. Unlike Esther, Joan has been eager for Buddy to bring his mother to visit at the hospital. Thus, Esther now knows that Joan is a reminder "of what I had been, and what I had been through." Joan's burial, then, signifies an aspect of Esther's new freedom, for what Esther buries at Joan's funeral is a part of her old, captive self.

Another symbol of Esther's new freedom is her diaphragm. As she points out, its acquisition frees her from the fear of unwanted pregnancy with its several undesirable consequences. She is no longer a sexual victim; even though her fear of marriage persists, she may now control her own fate. And the liberation afforded by this new control permits Esther to come to terms with her sexual identity. Able now to put aside the blandishments of her mother and Mrs. Willard, Esther is free to shed the virginity which has been such an intolerable psychological burden to her old self. She thus will be able to resolve the ambivalence which has so destructively divided her; the division of character represented by the former, oppressed Esther and her wish-fulfilling Elly Higginbottom is no longer necessary. Significantly, as Esther narrates the particulars of her tryst with Irwin, on whom she practices her "new, normal personality," she fails to mention the name by which Irwin called her. Surely she is no longer Elly, even though this experience is a sexual one. In leaving her narrator nameless, Plath represents the narrator's new wholeness, for she is not now the old Esther, either. She is truly, as she observes, "my own woman."

Thus renewed, Esther awaits her expected dismissal from the hospital. She has been, as she puts it, "born twice— patched, retreaded and approved for the road." The reader may safely assume that Esther's recovery is complete. Her prognosis seems good; the "new, normal personality" with which she now meets the world may well be sufficiently strong to resist future breakdown. Indeed, at the time when she actually tells this story, Esther is someone's wife and the mother of a baby; she is, she says, "all right," and she uses some of the free gifts from her chaotic summer in New York as toys for her child.

A Note of Warning

There is, however, a note of warning also sounded at the novel's close. A retreaded tire, surely, can come apart more readily than a new one. Further, Esther the narrator-character asks: "How did I know that someday—at college, in Europe, somewhere, anywhere—the bell jar, with its stifling distortions, wouldn't descend again?" Perhaps this question offers further corroboration of Esther's new, realistic self. On the other hand, we may hear in this question the voice of Esther's autobiographical creator, for whom the prognosis is dark indeed. Like the adult Esther who is recreating this narrative, Sylvia Plath is married and a mother. She is also "in Europe" (no mere coincidence that Esther the narrator-character should include such reference in her comment); she has suffered ill health, and her marriage is troubled. And, as we now know, for Sylvia Plath the bell jar did "descend again." Only months after the novel was accepted for publication, its author attempted suicide for a second and final time.

The Bell Jar Examines the Public and Private Worlds of Madness

Mason Harris

Mason Harris is a literary critic and professor of English at Simon Fraser University in Canada.

Many critics consider The Bell Jar *less artistically satisfying than the poetry of Sylvia Plath's* Ariel, *explains Harris in the following viewpoint. However,* The Bell Jar *succeeds as something that* Ariel *does not even attempt—to plumb not only the private world of madness but to lay bare the stifling culture that bred psychosis, Harris contends. Plath has crafted a scathing and accurate description of the oppressive culture of the 1950s and the chilling impact it had on a sensitive young woman, Harris asserts.*

There is a general tendency to view Sylvia Plath's only novel as an immature and artistically flawed piece of catharsis, useful as background to the lyrics but not up to par for the author of *Ariel*. This rating of the novel is supported by the author herself, who, as we learn in the "Biographical Note," explained to her mother that

> What I've done is to throw together events from my own life, fictionalizing to add color—it's a pot boiler really, but I think it will show how isolated a person feels when he is suffering a breakdown. . . . I've tried to picture my world and the people in it as seen through the distorting lens of a bell jar. . . . My second book will show the same world as seen through the eyes of health.

Mason Harris, "The Bell Jar," *West Coast Review*, vol. 8, October, 1973, pp. 54–56.
Copyright © by Mason Harris. All rights reserved. Reproduced by permission.

The Bell Jar Accurately Reflects the Oppressive Fifties

Her mother thought this admission amply justified blocking publication of the novel in the U.S. on the grounds that it contained unkind caricatures of a number of people "whom Sylvia loved" when she was sane. However, authors' opinions of their own work are notoriously suspect, Sylvia's here in particular. Firstly, it would seem that she is trying to mollify in advance the wounded feelings that her mother would experience when she read the novel and found that she was one of the caricatures. Also the plan for a "healthy" novel smacks of that brisk, determinedly cheerful, efficient woman Sylvia strove to appear in her everyday life, but fortunately not in her writing. Does any of her best work seem healthy, or even tell us what health is?

Perhaps as a poet Sylvia felt some contempt for the limitations of prose. While the novel seems as morbidly self-obsessed as the final poems it can hardly, as straightforward narrative, score *Ariel's* extraordinary breakthroughs in language and imagery. However, the novel also achieves something that intense confessional lyrics cannot: the poems dredge a private sickness which seems to arise only from the personal past while the novel throws open the social dimension of madness, indicating the culture in which the heroine has grown up, or rather which prevents her from doing so. Nowhere have I found so forceful a depiction of what it was like to be an adolescent in the stifling, hermetically-sealed world of the [President Dwight D.] Eisenhower 'Fifties. The "distorted lens" of madness gives an authentic vision of a period which exalted the most oppressive ideal of reason and stability.

Esther Greenwood, narrator and thinly-disguised version of Sylvia, is a brilliant straight-A student at an ivy-league Eastern women's college (Sylvia graduated *summa* from Smith). With the uncertainty attendant on compulsive drives she secretly suspects, despite all evidence to the contrary, that she is really quite stupid and ignorant and will someday be found out. As the novel opens in the summer of her Junior year she is in New York City as prize-winning guest editor of a leading fashion magazine (*Mademoiselle* in real life) experiencing, along with twelve other lucky girls, a publicity-stunt tour of the fashion world at its most superficial (the "Note" gives a sample of some deliciously awful prose Sylvia turned out for the mag). Esther forlornly reflects that this is a great opportunity for a girl of such limited means, and that she is supposed to be having the time of her life. The witty satire of the first half of the novel acquires darker meaning as the heroine (like Sylvia) lapses into madness and makes a most determined suicide attempt (far more thorough and apparently foolproof than the one which succeeded ten years later).

Plath Shows Society's Complicity in Madness

If this novel goes less deeply into psychotic experience than Hannah Green's *I Never Promised You A Rose Garden* or Janet Frame's *Faces in the Water* it also does a much more complete job of relating the heroine's madness to her social world. Esther's collapse is precipitated by the discovery of an inner deathliness concealed under the glossy surface of New York and her own compulsive drive to achievement. Because they are so personal, many of the poems of *Ariel* seem liable to explanation in classic Freudian formulae, but here something more is demanded. Granted that Esther-Sylvia suffered from fixation on her childhood relation to her parents, we also must ask how failure to find any feasible road to maturity contributed to her illness. Her longing to regress permeates the novel, but might not regression be partly the result of the apparent impossibility of further development?

In New York Esther acknowledges the inadequacy of the compulsive achievement which dominated her childhood and adolescence, yet cannot find a mature identity to replace it:

Sylvia Plath in 1961, two years before her death. © Photo Researchers.

"The one thing I was good at was winning scholarships and prizes, and that era was coming to an end. I felt like a race-horse in a world without racetracks . . . ". In a significantly mechanical metaphor she sees her life as a no thoroughfare: "I saw the years of my life spaced along a road in the form of telephone poles, threaded together by wires. I counted one, two, three . . . nineteen telephone poles, and then the wires dangled into space, and try as I would, I couldn't see a single pole beyond the nineteenth." [Psychologist] Erik Erikson has described the transition from childhood to maturity as a dar-ing leap across an abyss; the heroine of *The Bell Jar* finds only a cliff edge with nothing beyond.

The relation between regression and stifled development is particularly evident in the narrator's use of baby-images—central also to the poetry but developed with special clarity here. Pleasant baby-images are associated with the joys of re-gression but the novel is also haunted by the nightmare image of a fetus in a bottle—to which she was first introduced by her medical student boyfriend. This aspect of the baby be-comes a graphic expression of that sense of strangled develop-ment which is the other side of her tendency to regression. When after her recovery her mother says, "We'll act as if all this were a bad dream"; Esther thinks, "To the person in the bell jar, blank and stopped as a dead baby, the world itself is the bad dream." A particularly striking image links arrested growth to the world of the 'Fifties. From the pages of *Life Magazine* "The face of Eisenhower beamed up at me, bald and blank as the face of a fetus in a bottle." Esther also hates ba-bies because they represent the ideal of total domesticity, but sometimes longs to become a mother as a form of psychic suicide.

Esther Has No Healthy Outlet for Her Sexuality

Esther's breakdown comes after a series of unfortunate en-counters with sex in New York. The ensuing psychosis could partly be explained on the grounds of sexual repression and morbid attachment to her dead father, but it is also true that all the men she has known manifest variations on a consistently sick attitude toward women and marriage; since no remotely acceptable relationship is available her libido has nowhere to go but backwards.

The novel's sexuality is dominated by the American Mom as represented by her boyfriend's mother, Mrs. Willard, "with her heather-mixture tweeds and her sensible shoes and her wise, maternal maxims. Mr. Willard was her little boy, and his voice was high and clear, like a little boy's." The most oft-repeated of these maxims are "What a man wants is a mate and what a woman wants is infinite security,' and 'What a man is is an arrow into the future and what a woman is is the place the arrow shoots off from'." Her boyfriend Buddy, a "nice, clean boy" and a magnificent specimen of the male ideal of the 'Fifties in all his sentimental nobility, is particularly devoted to his mother. (When he sexlessly exhibits himself to Esther he explains that he wears net underpants because "'my mother says they wash easily'.")

The Oedipal split between pure love and degraded sexuality is made explicit by a Southern gentleman who laments to Esther that he can't have sex with a woman he truly loves: "it would be spoiled by thinking this woman too was just an animal like the rest, so if he loved anybody he would never go to bed with her. He'd go to a whore if he had to and keep the woman he loved free of all that dirty business." Esther gives up on him when he writes with incestuous ardor that she has "such a kind face, surprisingly like his older sister's."

In their big date at Yale, Buddy treats her "like a friend or cousin," kissing her only once gently behind the chem. lab— "'Wow, it makes me feel terrific to kiss you'." Esther has been much impressed with the necessity of remaining pure till her marriage night, and is outraged to find that while dating her the "clean" Buddy has fornicated at least thirty times with "some tarty waitress" who seduced him over the summer. Her more experienced friends explain that "most boys were like that" but Esther can't stand "the idea of a woman having to have a pure life and a man being able to have a double life, one pure and one not." She also begins to suspect that being the object of his "pure life" might become a bit oppressive: "I . . . remembered Buddy Willard saying in a sinister, knowing way that after I had children, I would feel differently, I wouldn't want to write poems any more." Perhaps "infinite security" is only a more painful form of suicide.

The most intense form of oedipal passion is demonstrated by Marco, a Latin woman-hater Esther meets at a party on her last evening in New York. He adores his first cousin—about to enter a nunnery—but can't marry her because of South American ideas about incest. When Esther offers the consolation that someday "'you'll love somebody else'" he responds by throwing her in the mud—"'Your dress is black and the dirt is black as well'"—spitting in her face, and trying to rape her while repeatedly hissing "'Slut!'" in her ear. She virtuously fights him off but he still insists, "'Sluts, all sluts. . . . Yes or no, it is all the same.'" It would seem that some violence also lurks in Buddy's love. He contracts T.B. [tuberculosis] and when Esther visits him at the sanatorium he resents her relative health and freedom. He forces her to ski down a dangerous slope and when she takes the inevitable spill informs her, smiling with a "queer, satisfied expression," that "'Your leg's broken in two places. You'll be stuck in a cast for months.'" These episodes seem so apt that one wonders whether they really happened that way, or were structured by the author to represent the inner truth of her experience—but since they are quite convincing this hardly matters.

Esther Resigns Herself to Prison

Thus personal relationships present no alternative to Esther's pursuit of straight A's. Hysterical and sexless devotion to the performance principle is exemplified by her friend Joan Gilling, a local "big wheel—president of her class and a physics major and the college hockey champion." Joan, who later turns out to be a Lesbian, dates Buddy because she so admires his mother. After learning of Esther's suicide attempt Joan becomes inspired to try it herself and winds up at the same asylum, where Esther sees her as "the beaming double of my old best self." Joan brings along all her schoolbooks, studies Freud, plans to become a psychiatrist, and finally hangs herself. At her funeral Esther finds some consolation in the fact that she herself has escaped this fate, but the reader knows that her apparent recovery is only a reprieve.

This novel is enclosed in many prisons, all expanded forms of the bell jar. The ladies in "Belsize," the "best" ward of Esther's exclusive hospital, put on a good imitation of upper middle class living: "What was there about us, in Belsize, so different from the girls playing bridge and gossiping and studying in the college to which I would return? Those girls, too, sat under bell jars of a sort." During her summer in New York the Rosenbergs are electrocuted[1] and Esther "couldn't help wondering what it would be like, being burnt alive along all your nerves." Later in a seedy private mental hospital she is punished for madness by shock therapy incompetently (or sadistically) administered: "with each flash a great jolt drubbed me till I thought my bones would break and the sap fly out of me like a split plant. I wondered what terrible thing it was that I had done." The parents of Esther's world seem to feel that mental and even physical illness arises from weak moral character. Esther's mother makes her become a volunteer worker in local hospitals because "the cure for thinking too much about yourself was helping somebody who was worse off than you." Buddy's father "simply couldn't stand the sight of sickness and especially his own son's sickness, because he thought all sickness was sickness of the will."

---

1. Ethel and Julius Rosenberg were American Communists executed for treason for passing nuclear secrets to the Soviets in 1953. The case was controversial and ongoing in the media.

In the end Esther's cure seems to consist more of resignation to prison than escape from it. If madness was precipitated by a demand for something better than the compulsive past, recovered sanity seems a depressing return to her "old best self" because nothing better has been found. Esther's coldly calculated plan to lose her viriginity ends in a freak hemorrage which seems to comment on the fallacy of trying to will an emotional experience. Sylvia once described *The Bell Jar* as "an autobiographical apprentice work which I had to write in order to free myself from the past." Though better than this the novel did not grant the self understanding that would free her, nor did the even more brilliant *Ariel*. On the other hand if madness is a form of insight and itself a comment on its causes, then effective expression of it may achieve success in art, if not in life. In its forceful linking of private to public madness *The Bell Jar* not only adds a new dimension to the poetry but deserves to be considered a major work in its own right.

The Bell Jar Relates a Girl's Search for Identity

Marjorie G. Perloff

Marjorie G. Perloff is Sadie Dernham Patek professor emerita of humanities at Stanford University.

The story of The Bell Jar *is the attempt of a young woman to create an authentic identity instead of living up to society's expectations, states Perloff in the following viewpoint. Esther becomes psychotic because the demands of society are oppressive. Images of physical and mental illness throughout the novel suggest the unhealthy state of the human condition, Perloff writes. By the end of the novel, with the help of her therapist, Esther has learned to simply be herself, Perloff concludes.*

In *The Divided Self*, [Scots psychiatrist] R.D. Laing gives this description of the split between inner self and outer behavior that characterizes the schizoid personality: "The 'inner self' is occupied in phantasy and observation. It observes the processes of perception and action. Experience does not impinge . . . directly on this self, and the individual's acts are the provinces of a false-self system." The condition Laing describes is precisely that of Esther at the beginning of [*The Bell Jar*]. For example, when Jay Cee, the *Ladies' Day* editor, asks Esther, "What do you have in mind after you graduate?" Esther's inner self observes her own external response with strange detachment: "'I don't really know,' *I heard myself say.* . . . It sounded true, and I recognized it, the way you recognize some nondescript person that's been hanging around your door for ages and then suddenly comes up and introduces himself as

Marjorie G. Perloff, "A Ritual for Being Born Twice: Sylvia Plath's *The Bell Jar*," *Contemporary Literature*, vol. 13, Autumn 1972, pp. 507–22. Copyright © The Board of Regents of the University of Wisconsin System. All rights reserved. Reproduced by permission.

your real father and looks exactly like you, so you know he really is your father, and the person you thought all your life was your father is a sham." In a similarly detached way, Esther listens to the words of Elly Higginbottom, the name she has suddenly and inexplicably adopted in order to cope with the stranger who has picked her up on Times Square. But while Elly prattles on, Esther's real self becomes "a small dot" and finally "a hole in the ground."

The Bell Jar Is a Quest for Identity

If we take the division of Esther's self as the motive or starting point of the novel's plot, the central action of *The Bell Jar* may be described as the attempt to heal the fracture between inner self and false-self systems so that a real and viable identity can come into existence. But because, as Laing reminds us, "everyone in some measure wears a mask," Esther's experience differs from that of so-called "normal" girls in degree rather than in kind. It is simply a stylized or heightened version of the young American girl's quest to forge her own identity, to be herself rather than what others expect her to be.

The dust jacket image of Esther as the brilliant, beautiful, successful girl who is somehow "going under" is, to begin with, wholly misleading. The Esther others see is, from the very first page of the novel, an elaborate contrivance, an empty shell: the fashionable Smith girl with her patent leather bag and matching pumps, the poised guest editor, brainy but no bookworm, equally at home on the dance floor or behind the typewriter. The novel's flashbacks make clear that Esther has always played those roles others have wanted her to play. For her mother, she has been the perfect *good girl*, "trained at a very early age and . . . no trouble whatsoever." For Mr. Manzi, her physics professor, she is the ideal student, even though she secretly loathes the "hideous, cramped, scorpion-lettered formulas" with which he covers the blackboard. For Buddy Wil-lard, her one serious boyfriend, she is all sweetness and acquiescence. . . .

The scenes in the present which lead up to Esther's break-down reveal the same pattern. For Doreen, Esther wears the mask of tough cookie, willing to be picked up by strangers on downtown street corners. For Betsy from the Middle West, she is the fun girl who likes fur shows. For Constantin, the simul-taneous interpreter at the UN, she is a no-nonsense type, pre-paring for a career as a war correspondent. Perhaps the final action committed by Esther's external self is the terrible forced smile she bestows on the *Ladies' Day* photographers (see the photograph on the dust jacket), a smile that suddenly dis-solves in tears. Here the false-self system finally crumbles, and the old Esther must die before she can be reborn as a human being.

Recurrent mirror and light images measure Esther's de-scent into the stale air beneath the bell jar. In the first chapter, when Esther returns from Lenny's apartment and enters the mirrored elevator of the Amazon Hotel, she notices "a big, smudgy-eyed Chinese woman staring idiotically into my face. It was only me, of course. I was appalled to see how wrinkled and used up I looked." As the self becomes increasingly dis-embodied, the reflection in the mirror gradually becomes a stranger. Having symbolically killed her false self by throwing her clothes to the winds from the hotel rooftop, Esther rides home on the train to the Boston suburbs and notes that "The face in the mirror looked like a sick Indian." But the "two di-agonal lines of dried blood" on her cheeks do not perturb her, for her body no longer seems real. Appearances do not count—Esther no longer washes or changes clothes or puts on make-up—and yet she is constantly afraid of being recognized by others. "In a world full of dangers," writes Laing, "to be a potentially seeable object is to be constantly exposed to danger. . . . The obvious defence against such a danger is to make oneself invisible in one way or another." Thus Esther, hiding behind the bedroom shutters, feels Dodo Conway's "gaze pierce through the white clapboard and pink wallpaper roses and uncover me"; she finds the early morning light so oppressive that she crawls beneath the mattress to escape it, but it seems as if "the mattress was not heavy enough," and, after twenty-one sleepless nights, Esther thinks that "the most beautiful thing in the world must be shadow." Only by returning to the womb in the shape of the basement crawl space at her mother's house and then gulping down a bottle of sleeping pills, does she hope to find the "dark . . . thick as velvet," which is the darkness of death.

Esther's body is recalled to life fairly easily, but the self that emerges from her suicide attempt is hopelessly disembodied. When she looks into the mirror the hospital nurse reluctantly brings her, Esther thinks, "It wasn't a mirror at all, but a picture. You couldn't tell whether the person in the picture was a man or a woman, because their hair was shaved off and sprouted in bristly chicken-feather tufts all over their head. One side of the person's face was purple. . . . The most startling thing about the face was its supernatural conglomeration of bright colors." It is only when she smiles at this funny face, and "the mouth in the mirror cracked into a grin," that Esther is reminded of her identity and sends the mirror crashing to the floor. It will take a long time to pick up the pieces.

The Bell Jar Analyzes the Problems Women Face

But why is Esther's inner self so precarious, so disembodied in the first place? Why must she invent such an elaborate set of masks with which to face the world? To label Esther as "schizophrenic" and leave it at that does not take us very far. For Sylvia Plath's focus in *The Bell Jar* is not on mental illness per se, but on the relationship of Esther's private psychosis to her larger social situation. Indeed, her dilemma seems to have a great deal to do with being a woman in a society whose guidelines for women she can neither accept nor reject. It is beautifully ironic that Sylvia Plath, who never heard of Women's Liberation and would be unlikely to join The Movement were she alive today, has written one of the most acute analyses of the feminist problem that we have in contemporary fiction. What makes *The Bell Jar* so moving—and often so marvelously funny—is that the heroine is just as innocent as she is frighteningly perceptive. Far from rejecting the stereotyped world which she inhabits—a world whose madness often seems much more intense than Esther's own—she is determined to conquer it. Fulfillment, the novel implies, must come here or not at all; there is no better world around the corner or across the ocean. Thus Esther's quest for identity centers around her repeated attempts—sometimes funny but always painful—to find both a female model whom she can emulate and a man whom she need not despise. If this quest does not lead to a Brave New World of happy liberated women, we need not be disappointed. Like [writer Anton] Chekhov, Sylvia Plath knows that the novelist's job is not to solve problems but to diagnose them correctly. . . .

Illness Is a Metaphor for a Sick Society

Throughout the novel, Sylvia Plath emphasizes the curious similarity of physical and mental illness as if to say that both are symbolic of a larger condition which is our life today. *The Bell Jar* opens with the following sentence: "It was a queer, sultry summer, the summer they electrocuted the Rosenbergs, and I didn't know what I was doing in New York."[1] This reference to electrocution sets the scene for everything that is to come: before the novel is over, Esther herself will know only too well what it feels like to be "burned alive all along your nerves." The terrible electric shock therapy that Dr. Gordon

1. Ethel and Julius Rosenberg were American Communists executed in 1953 for passing nuclear secrets to the Soviets. The case was controversial and had ongoing media coverage.

makes her undergo is a frightening counterpart of the Rosenbergs' punishment; "I wondered," Esther thinks as she goes under, "what terrible thing it was that I had done." Even the bare room in which the shock treatment is administered resembles the Rosenbergs' prison cell: the windows are barred, and "everything that opened and shut was fitted with a key-hole so it could be locked up."

From the start, when Esther contemplates the terrible fate of the Rosenbergs, sickness is everywhere around her; it begins when Esther finds the drunken Doreen lying on the floor of the hotel corridor: "A jet of brown vomit flew from her mouth and spread in a large puddle at my feet." Here, Sylvia Plath suggests, is the real picture of the desirable debutante, whose smiling photographs grace the pages of the fashion magazines. . . .

In the world of *The Bell Jar*, no one is exempt from illness. Even Buddy Willard, the all-American boy who radiates good health, develops tuberculosis and has to spend a winter in a sanatorium. . . .

Sylvia Plath is no silly sentimentalist; she knows quite well that her heroine *is* different from most college girls, that her bell jar is less fragile, less easy to remove than theirs. But the external or official distinction between madness and sanity, she suggests in her linkage of physical and mental illness, is largely illusory. When, to take the novel's most striking example, Esther breaks her leg skiing, Buddy—and the world at large—regard her broken leg as the most normal of accidents. Yet Esther's account of her mental state as she plummets down the slope suggests that she is never closer to insanity than at this particular moment. A novice skier, she suddenly conceives an overwhelming desire to fly off into "the great, gray eye of the sky." Like the ecstatic speaker of [her poem] "Ariel," who longs to make the "Suicidal" leap "Into the red/ Eye, the cauldron of morning," Esther longs for the annihilation of death. "People and trees receded on either hand like the dark sides of a tunnel as I hurtled on to the still, bright point at the end of it, the pebble at the bottom of the well, the white sweet baby cradled in its mother's belly." Yet this suicidal leap earns Esther no more than a plaster cast, whereas her later, not unrelated suicide attempt precipitates her admission to the dangerous ward of the hospital.

The plot of *The Bell Jar* moves from physical sickness (the ptomaine poisoning) to mental illness and back to the physical, culminating in Esther's hemorrhage. The arrangement of incidents implies that all illness is to be viewed as part of the same spectrum: disease, whether mental or physical, is an index to the human inability to cope with an unlivable situation. For who can master a world where the Testing Kitchens of the leading women's magazine poison all of its guest editors, where a reputable psychiatrist asks a girl, on the verge of suicide, whether there is a WAC [Women's Army Corps] station at her college?

Esther Learns to Be Herself

But Esther does come back to life. At the end of *The Bell Jar*, her external situation has not appreciably changed—she has found neither a lover nor her future vocation—but now she can view that situation differently. Having passed through death, she learns, with the help of Dr. Nolan, to forge a new identity. It is important to note that Dr. Nolan, the only wholly admirable woman in the novel, is also the only woman whom Esther never longs to imitate or to resemble. The point is that Dr. Nolan serves not as model but as anti-model; she is the instrument whereby Esther learns to be, not some other woman, but herself. The new Esther takes off the mask: she openly rejects Joan's lesbian advances; she can cope with Irwin as well as with Buddy. Best of all, the world of nature, distorted and fragmented in the opening pages of the novel when Esther walks through the "granite canyons" of Manhattan, is no longer inaccessible. Shovelling Buddy's car out of the snow,

Esther watches with pleasure as the sun emerges from the clouds: "Pausing in my work to overlook that pristine expanse, I felt the same profound thrill it gives me to see trees and grassland waist-high under flood water—as if the usual order of the world had shifted slightly, and entered a new phase."

As if the usual order of the world had shifted slightly. . . . When Esther pauses on the threshold of the room where the hospital board is waiting to pass final sentence on her, she still sees her future as a series of "question marks", but she has learned something very important. Isolation, Sylvia Plath suggests, the terrible isolation Esther feels when, one by one, her props crumble, is paradoxically the result of negating one's own separateness. The hardest thing in the world to do—and it is especially hard when one is young, female, and highly gifted—is simply to be oneself. Only when Esther recognizes that she will never be a Jody, a Jay Cee, a Doreen, or a Mrs. Guinea, that she will never marry a Buddy Willard, a Constantin, or a Dr. Gordon, that she wants no lesbian affairs with a Joan or a Dee Dee—does the bell jar lift, letting Esther once again breathe "the circulating air." As a schizophrenic, Esther is, of course, a special case, but her intensity of purpose, her isolation, her suffering, and finally her ability to survive it all with a sense of humor, make her an authentic, indeed an exemplary heroine of the seventies. . . .

Esther's landscape, with its confusing assortment of cadavers and diamonds, thermometers and beans, is, in heightened form, *our* landscape. When [Norwegian playwright Henrik] Ibsen's Nora [in *A Doll's House*] slammed the door of her doll's house and embarked on a new life, she nobly refused to take with her any of Torvald's property. The New Woman, I would posit, will not let men off that easily. Esther, having undergone emergency treatment for the hemorrhage induced by Irwin's lovemaking, calmly sends him the bill.

The Bell Jar Chronicles a Search for Authenticity

Susan Coyle

Literary critic Susan Coyle has taught English at the University of Akron in Ohio.

Sylvia Plath uses a variety of metaphors in The Bell Jar *to tell how Esther Greenwood lost and then regained her identity, explains Coyle in the following viewpoint. Esther finds herself surrounded with negative role models for wife, mother, and sexual being. Rejecting these images, she despairs of finding an authentic identity and makes multiple attempts at suicide. At the end of the novel, with the help of her therapist, Esther accepts that she must satisfy herself, not others, and is reborn as an integrated personality.*

Sylvia Plath's *The Bell Jar* is replete with metaphor: metaphor of death, of alienation, of losing one's self and, later, regaining that self. From the outset of the novel, where the narrator, Esther Greenwood, is obsessed with thoughts of cadavers, pickled babies, and the execution of the Rosenbergs[1], to the ending, where Esther consciously and triumphantly goes through a metaphoric rebirth, Plath takes the reader on a remarkable tour of metaphor. Through this use of metaphor, the reader comes to see, feel, and know Esther's world intimately and vividly. Essentially, the novel chronicles Esther's quest for identity, for authenticity, in a world that seems hostile to everything she wants. . . .

1. Ethel and Julius Rosenberg were executed in 1953 for passing nuclear secrets to the Soviets. The case was controversial and had ongoing media coverage.

Susan Coyle, "Images of Madness and Retrieval: An Exploration of Metaphor in *The Bell Jar*," *Studies in American Fiction*, vol. 12, Autumn 1984, pp. 161–74. Copyright © 1984 by John Hopkins University Press. All rights reserved. Reproduced by permission.

Plath Uses Metaphor to Show Esther's Search for Identity

Throughout the novel, Esther is known most tellingly through her use of metaphor. Plath's use of imagery changes markedly prior to and after the suicide attempt that leads to the asylum; the images of pre-breakdown are almost unrelievedly negative. The novel contains veritable cadences of death and remarkable images showing the hostility of the world around Esther, but the metaphors of primary interest are the ones that concern self, that reflect her states of mind. In the pre-breakdown part of the novel, Esther's sexual experiences are all somewhat dislocating: she cannot define herself as a sexual being. The patterns that she sees of marriage and motherhood make her loathe more than desire either of these accepted institutions. Esther's negative view of herself as an individual is reflected in her choices of metaphor; these images are frequently very physical, tied to her body. Slowly, she becomes increasingly dissociated from herself, until a sense of the "other" is clearly established, a dark side of herself who acts almost without Esther's volition. Contingently, there is a rebellion of matter: things (clothes in a pile, words on a page) that were previously predictable and inert now acquire an active and malevolent force of their own, a force the diminishing Esther is powerless to control. Language symbols fall apart for the protagonist, and nothing is left to hold on to.

After the turning point of the novel, which certainly does not conform to the traditional idea of an "adventure," unless it is a macabre adventure, these groups of metaphors change radically. Some do not go through any transformation; they die with Esther's madness. Others, such as the body images, change and become more positive, if less physical. In the "recovery" phase of *The Bell Jar*, Esther is known more through her actions and overt assertions, and the metaphors connected with these. The obsessive sense of self has been left behind, and the new self is more concerned with what she will be *do-*

ing. Through her own effort, with Dr. Nolan's help, Esther ultimately forms an authentic self and manages to grow up rather than down. . . .

Esther Unable to Find a Role in a Repressive Society

At the outset of the novel, Esther is an outstanding student, successful and seemingly full of possibility. She sees her life as a metaphoric fig tree, offering multiple possibilities on every branch, yet she is unable to take even one of the figs. In her perception,

> . . . one fig was a husband and a happy home and children, and another fig was a famous poet and another fig was a brilliant professor, and another fig was Ee Gee, the amazing editor, and another fig was Europe and Africa and South America, and another fig was Constantin and Socrates and Attila and a pack of other lovers with queer names and off-beat professions, and another fig was an Olympic lady crew champion, and beyond and above these figs were many more figs I couldn't quite make out.
>
> I saw myself sitting in the crotch of this fig tree, starving to death, just because I couldn't make up my mind which one of the figs I would choose.

Esther is "starving" not simply from indecision but also from an increasing sense of alienation from self and alienation from the world and her potential goals. The husband and children are scathingly undercut by the possibilities that Buddy and Mrs. Willard present. The career potentials are effectively undermined when she becomes unable to read or write. And the lovers become virtually impossible when she fails to gain a sense of herself as a sexual being. She either cannot get to the figs (editor, sex, poet) or the figs no longer represent viable alternatives (marriage, family).

In "The Divided Woman and Generic Doubleness in *The Bell Jar*," Gayle Whittier writes that "Esther Greenwood's primary identity is that of an intellectual woman. According to her society's standards, an 'intellectual woman' is herself a cultural contradiction in terms, a disharmonious combination of biology and intelligence. It is in part from this sense of herself as a living paradox that Esther grows increasingly depressed." Indeed, Esther is struggling to find a synthesis in her life that will allow her to combine her intelligence and ambition with fitting into a socially accepted role. She has been told that she should want marriage and motherhood and is moving toward both of these through Buddy Willard. Yet when she imagines what it might actually be like, she recoils. Her mother and Mrs. Willard are the two role models she has, and she does not want to be like either one. Mrs. Greenwood "never had a minute's peace" in her marriage, and from Mrs. Willard's example she infers that men really want women to be rugs under their feet, ever obliging, ever ready to subordinate themselves. Buddy Willard, as the prospective groom, husband, father, is more than willing to encourage Esther to lay down herself and marry him. In Gayle Whittier's words, "he regards marriage as a killing cure which will halve Esther's tense union of mind and body, leaving only the flesh." Esther sees that he will benefit from the union, but she will suffer and concludes that "maybe it was true that when you were married and had children it was like being brainwashed, and afterward you went about numb as a slave in some private, totalitarian way." She faces this prospect with terror and abhorrence. Because of Buddy's suggested life for her, and other models around her, she is also less than ambivalent about motherhood.

While the society's norms have taught her that it is a great good, she sees the novel's actual birth in negative terms and focuses more on the dead fetuses in jars than she does on any live babies. Plath's portrait of Dodo Conway, her chief example of motherhood, is scathing. The very name "Dodo" is insulting. Dodo is forever pregnant, with a "grotesque, protruding stomach," children swarming around her feet, and physically looks like "a sparrow egg perched on a duck egg." After this unflatterng description, Esther says that Dodo raises her children on "Rice Krispies, peanut-butter-and-marshmallow sandwiches, vanilla ice cream," and milk. There is an insipid, mindlessly fecund aura around the woman, and one has a sense that she is more like fertile eggs about to hatch than like a person. Esther concludes: "Children make me sick." Through her views on marriage and motherhood, Esther is understandably alienated from these two institutions. To submit to them will leave her, metaphorically, as a rug, and a sick rug at that.

Esther's Sexual Experiences Are Unfulfilling

Sexually, Esther cannot find her place in the world. Her sexual metaphors are vivid, sometimes hilarious, and sometimes touched with pathos. When Buddy Willard, the ostensible object of her desire, undresses in front of her in a passionless sort of show-and-tell, she looks at his genitals and thinks of "turkey neck and turkey gizzards." Understandably, she is very depressed. When Buddy suggests that she reciprocate in the undressing display, she refuses and again finds a metaphor to suit the occasion: the suggested disrobing would be tantamount to having her college Posture Picture taken in the nude. Her lack of feeling has much more to do with Buddy than with herself. She *wants* to be a sexual person, but Buddy is unquestionably the wrong person for her. Adding to this confusion, another college boy tells her that having sex (albeit with a whore) is as "boring as going to the toilet." After the negative and thwarting sexual views of the college boys, Esther encounters another sexually warped but even more dangerous man, Marco the misogynist. He is described in a remarkable combination of images: animal, god, and machine. His smile reminds Esther of a snake striking. Like a savage animal, he later tears her dress with his teeth. She concludes, "women-haters were like gods: invulnerable and chock-full of power."

When she punches him in the nose, "it was like hitting the steel plate of a battleship." And this twisted type of man, the animal-machine, adds to Esther's ill-fated and devastating quasi-sexual encounters. So this fig too seems to be downed, falling withered to the ground. While she has a desire to be a sexual woman, the list of lovers seems to evaporate when she is unable to make any kind of meaningful sexual connection.

In terms of sexuality, marriage, and motherhood, Esther is faced with the growing up grotesque archetype. If she takes the routes which her society approves, she will be personally unsatisfied, if not dismal. She is in search of an authenticity but is unable to find it. She wants to both go by the rules and satisfy herself, and it is no wonder that the pressures within her begin to mount and eventually become overwhelming. . . .

Esther is having difficulty placing herself in the world, which is reflected in metaphor, and her self-image is also readily discernible through imagery. In the pre-breakdown narration there are virtually no positive self-images and very few positive images of the world around Esther. . . .

Many of the metaphors of self are quite physical, describing her body. When Esther is sick with food poisoning, she is "limp as a wet leaf" and the white tiles of the bathroom make a "glittering white torture chamber" which threatens to crush her to pieces. Again and again the same theme occurs: her body is helpless, and the world is assaulting it. . . .

During the skiing flashback, Plath uses a metaphor that summarizes Esther's early attitude toward herself and the world. For a few seconds, as she speeds down the hill, Esther is happy. The happiness seems to come from two impulses: self-destruction (she might die on her way down) and rebirth (rushing down the hill is like rushing toward one's birth). Yet, ironically, at this exhilarating moment, she is knocked unconscious. As she slowly comes back to consciousness, her assessment is that "piece by piece, as at the strokes of a dull godmother's wand, the old world sprang back into positon."

A fig tree. Susan Coyle describes a number of metaphors that Plath uses in The Bell Jar, *including the fig tree. Esther Greenwood views her life as a metaphorical fig tree that is full of possibilities; unable to choose among the figs, she starves while they all shrivel and fall to the ground.* © Richard T. Nowitz/Corbis.

Esther's possibilities for happiness simply do not lie within this world. Self-destruction would deliver her *from* the world, and since the rebirth that excites her is momentary and abstract, it is not very viable. The world as she knows it comes back to her, a gift from a dull godmother.

Esther Creates a Double to Kill Her Negative Personality

Aside from her negative view of self and alienation from the world, Esther encounters yet another problem—dissociation from herself. Whenever Esther meets men who might provide sexual adventure, she uses the phony name Elly Higginbottom. Doreen knows this, and early in the novel Doreen and the Amazon night maid are outside Esther's door, one calling "Elly, Elly, Elly" and the other calling "Miss Greenwood, Miss Greenwood, Miss Greenwood." Esther, awakened by these calls, is perplexed at them, thinking that it sounds "as if I had a split personality or something." This early episode foreshadows, on a superficial level, the otherness and doubleness that will occur within Esther. The Esther of *The Bell Jar* has never felt at ease with her body, and so it seems appropriate that the otherness begins with her body. It is as if the foreigner in her blood rises and betrays her. When she is talking on the phone about the writing course that she was not accepted for, she realizes that "my voice sounded strange and hollow in my ears." That in itself is not particularly odd, but only a few lines later the voice is seemingly no longer hers: "The hollow voice" answers the girl on the phone, and Esther listens to it as she would to another person's voice. Just after this, she tries to make another phone call, but again her body is behaving strangely: "My hand advanced a few inches, then retreated and fell limp. I forced it toward the receiver again, but again it stopped short, as if it had collided with a pane of glass." Things are beginning to be out of her control; her hand acts as if it had volition.

This revolt in the flesh occurs at the same time as the failure of language: the breakdown has begun in earnest. When she visits her aunt the doctor, the division within her becomes more malevolent: "I tried to speak in a cool, calm way, but the zombie rose up in my throat and choked me off." By the time she goes to Dr. Gordon, she knows that things are definitely amiss and hopes that he can help her "to be myself again." Plath creates a sense of duality and horrific doubleness. Some other has arisen and taken control of her, and whoever she is, she is not herself. Dr. Gordon does not help her; his shock treatments only exacerbate the problem.

In three of her suicidal forays—razors, strangulation, and drowning—there are contrasting examples of the double within. When she is in the bathroom, contemplating death in the bath, she has a startling realization:

> But when it came right down to it, the skin of my wrist
> looked so white and defenseless that I couldn't do it. It was

> as if what I wanted to kill wasn't in that skin or the thin
> blue pulse that jumped under my thumb, but somewhere
> else, deeper, more secret, a whole lot harder to get at.

What she wants to kill is not herself but the other within her. In a surprising turnabout, Esther exhibits almost a tenderness toward her physical self and does not want to kill it. She is divided, wanting to kill *something* within herself but not wanting to kill *all* of herself.

When she tries to strangle herself (humorously enough, with the silk cord from her mother's bathrobe), she runs into another problem. Her internal dilemmas seem to be solved, and she is determined to really do the deed, but her body sabotages her. Just as she feels herself about to lose consciousness, her hands let go of the cord and she revives. She is annoyed with all the "little tricks" of her body, and resolves "I would simply have to ambush it with whatever sense I had left, or it would trap me in its stupid cage for fifty years." Similarly, when she decides to drown herself, she chooses a method of death with which her body will not cooperate. It keeps popping her back to the surface of the water, and her "heartbeat boomed like a dull motor in my ears. I am I am I am." The painful division is ever-present. When her mind is resolved to do away with the body, the body will not cooperate, and when the body allows for the possibility, her mind hesitates. This feeling of division and alienation from self, the world, and every possibility becomes overwhelming, and Esther devises a plan whereby she can successfully get rid of all the pain. She fails, of course, and ironically enough awakens to a face she does not recognize.

When Esther is in the crawl-space, she crouches "like a troll". Her next awareness is in the hospital, when her head rises, feeling like "the head of a worm." While in the hospital, the staff members look at her as if she were a "zoo animal" and speak to her as if she were "a dull child." There is also the first reference to the bell jar, which Esther is "sitting under . . .

stewing in my own sour air." Later, when Joan shows her the scrapbook of clippings about Esther, she notes with a kind of detachment that the picture shows her as a "long, limp blanket roll with a featureless cabbage head" being put into an ambulance. And here the intensely negative metaphors end. The dense, ferocious, and most moving metaphors are reserved for the earlier states of self when Esther is irretrievably alienated and depressed. The later images change and are much less physical, less concerned with her body and more concerned with action and the possibility of a more hospitable world around her.

The Ending Is Ambiguous

This is not to say that there is a sense of total resolution in the end of the novel, any unrealistic happy ending. At the end of the book, Esther says that she is "patched, retreaded, and approved for the road." This seems to be accurate, since the reader does not have a sense of her as a brand-new, unblemished tire but of one that has been painstakingly reworked, remade. Madness is still a potential threat; Esther's sexual achievement is not the blissful initiation that the reader would wish for her; everyone does not live happily ever after. But the steps that she does take toward defining herself in the world, the assertions and actions, however tentative, do lead her toward an authentic self that was previously impossible for her. . . .

Esther resolves her conflicts about her sexuality and motherhood by accepting how she genuinely feels and acting on those feelings. She realizes that she wants to have sexual relationships but that the chief drawback is "I've got a baby hanging over my head like a big stick, to keep me in line." She accepts her ostensibly unmaternal feelings, stating that "if I had to wait on a baby all day, I would go mad." As she climbs onto the gynecologist's examining table, she thinks "'I am climbing to freedom, freedom from fear, freedom from marrying the wrong person . . . freedom from the Florence Crittenden Homes [for unwed mothers],'" and later, when she has the diaphragm, asserts "I was my own woman." She also resolves the conflict about marriage, recognizing that if it means marrying someone like Buddy she does not want it at all. She says good-bye to him, and while she does not know who will marry her now that she has her own unorthodox "landscape," one has a sense that she is not particularly worried about it. She has a bright, if tentative, confidence in herself and is no longer belaboring the marriage issue.

Because Esther is integrating herself and losing the sense of otherness within, Joan becomes the objective correlative for this doubleness. At a relatively early point in the asylum, when Joan has town privileges while Esther does not, Esther feels that "Joan was the beaming double of my old best self, specially designed to follow and torment me." Later, when their positions reverse, Esther concludes that Joan's "thoughts and feelings seemed a wry, black image of my own." This double succeeds in killing herself, and Esther goes to her funeral with the puzzling thought that "I wondered what I thought I was burying." She seems to be burying her own dark side, seduced by death in the person of Joan. In another imagistic reprise from early in the novel, Esther, as survivor at the funeral of her dark side, listens to "the old brag of my heart. I am, I am, I am."

While the new Esther shovels snow for Buddy, she looks around her and feels a "profound thrill . . . as if the usual order of the world had shifted slightly, and entered a new phase." This can be contrasted with the earlier idea of a dull godmother forming the world. This time, the world and its possibilities seem bright, and if there has been a godmother, it has been jointly Esther herself and Dr. Nolan working to make the world, or Esther's perception of it, different. In the final scene, Esther goes to her interview with the doctors in a "red wool suit, flamboyant as my plans." The metaphor concerns plans for the future and not just physical self. Esther moves in her red suit into the room where the doctors wait, ready to determine her release. As she describes it, "the eyes and the faces all turned themselves toward me, and guiding myself by them, as by a magical thread, I stepped into the room." This is definitely a birth, or more accurately, a rebirth scene. Esther, dressed in a symbolically bloody color, is the focus of the scene, with the eyes of all the doctors on her. As a baby in the process of birthing would, she "guides" herself by them and is brought back to the world by their authority and help. The "magical thread" is analogous to an umbilical cord, but in this case it seems to be her own volition and self-command that allow her to step into the room, symbolically taking the responsibility and credit for her own rebirth.

The Bell Jar Illustrates Women's Limited Options

Mary Allen

Mary Allen is a literary critic.

In The Bell Jar *Esther Greenwood is both attracted to and repelled by the world of feminine contrivance she encounters in New York, Allen claims in the following viewpoint. Her attempts at suicide reflect her self-loathing; if society demands that she waste her intelligence on a trivial job, she might as well be dead. Esther's dilemma accurately reflects the situation facing women—there is no role open to them other than the conventional ones of wife and mother—Allen declares.*

No woman in American literature is quite so thoroughly repulsed by what women are as is Esther Greenwood. She is an unusually ambitious girl, successful in every apparent way with fifteen years of straight A's behind her, who has now won a contest to work for *Ladies' Day* fashion magazine in New York for one month in the summer. (Sylvia Plath won the award to work for *Mademoiselle* in 1953.) But what could be a thrilling experience is a deadening one, like all others in her adult life. The summer concludes with several suicide attempts, all made the more terrible to the reader by the fact of Plath's own suicide in 1963, one month after publication of *The Bell Jar.*

Esther Is Both Fascinated and Disgusted

Like [author] Joyce Carol Oates, Sylvia Plath is obsessed with images of blood. Both women see things disintegrating in a world filled with signs of death, where women find no hint of

Mary Allen, "Sylvia Plath's Defiance: *The Bell Jar*," in *Necessary Blankness: Women in Major American Fiction of the Sixties*. Champaign: University of Illinois Press, 1976, pp. 160–78. Copyright © 1976 by Mary Allen. All rights reserved. Reproduced by permission.

the romantic in their lives and are disgusted by their bodies. But one great difference between the two writers is the intimidation Oates's women feel in relation to outside forces in contrast with the disdain of Esther Greenwood, who projects much more of her own will, self-destructive as it is. If she cannot control what society expects of her, she does dramatically register her disgust for how she is supposed to live and how she is to look, which is perhaps the most overwhelming fact of herself a woman must cope with.

While she is not unattractive, Esther never considers herself a beauty and is overwhelmed by the world of fashion among the clientele of *Ladies' Day*. Like them she buys glossy patent leather shoes from Bloomingdale's, symbolic of the surfacy nature of style. She is at the same time repulsed and envious of girls who are bored by too many love affairs and who spend their days painting their fingernails and keeping up Bermuda tans. The Amazon Hotel, where only girls stay, is presumed by their mothers to keep them safely away from men, announcing an attitude held throughout *The Bell Jar* that men are polluters. Female conversation disgusts Esther, but she is sickeningly drawn to it. She is in awe of the glittery Doreen, who dwells on such trivia as the way she and her friends at college make pocketbook covers of the same material as their clothes so that each outfit matches. Esther confesses that "this kind of detail impressed me. It suggested a whole life of marvelous, elaborate decadence that attracted me like a magnet." Aware of her intrigue with what appalls her, Esther increasingly loathes herself, realizing the great extent to which her image of herself is based on the objects of fashion. A gift for each girl when she arrives in New York is a makeup kit, created exactly for a person of such-and-such a color, the first essential item in establishing her new life. Each girl is photographed carrying a prop to indicate her identity: an ear of corn for one who looks forward to being a farmer's wife, a gold-embroidered sari for another who plans on being a social

A magazine illustration from the 1950s. Options for women in the 1950s were largely confined to domestic roles. © Blue Latern Studio/Corbis.

worker in India. Before Esther leaves New York she mocks a suicide by abandoning her props, the fashionable clothes that have identified her, letting each item float down over the city from the top of her hotel as a way of renouncing the standards of fashion and also of obliterating herself. The climax of Esther's encounter with New York's world of fashion, dramatically proving it to be insidious, comes when a luncheon sponsored by *Ladies' Day* results in the ptomaine poisoning of all the girls who attend. . . .

Esther's Suicide Attempts Are Passive

In the midst of New York's activity and opportunity Esther enters a numbing depression, as though selection and will are unknown to her, having excelled only in the structured situation of the classroom. "I felt like a racehorse in a world without racetracks or a champion college footballer suddenly con-

fronted by Wall Street and a business suit." She is a figure
bumped from one hotel to another, incapable of steering herself. In her hotel room she flattens out on the bed trying to
think of people who have her phone number and who might
call, never considering the possibility of making the calls herself. Rather than attend a fashion show she wants only to stay
in bed all day or to lie on the grass in Central Park. Esther
considers herself "dealt" to the woman-hater Marco as his
blind date, who informs her that it makes no difference if she
cannot dance since it takes only one person to dance anyway.
All she must do is be on the dance floor with him. Esther has
always waited for men to fall in love with her; there is no
thought of affection for any of them. Her most decisive action
is the project to unload her virginity, but even in this she
merely reclines on the bed and lets it happen.

The situation of the college girl whose self-esteem hinges
on a phone call might not merit our attention here if it were
not that this stance remains basic in the woman. The passivity
that operates in Esther's view of herself as a girl continues in
her means of attempting suicide and in the desire for the ultimate passivity in death. Even the fact that she must take some
kind of action to accomplish her death is distressing to her,
doubly so because of her sense of incapacity. On one occasion
she tries bleeding herself with a razor in a warm bath, on the
advice of an ancient Roman, but she cannot tolerate the sight
of blood. On the calm day of a beach party she tries to drown,
diving down several times but popping back into the sunlight
from the force of the sea. She asks her timid date Cal how he
would try killing himself, and when he tells her he would use
a gun she figures "it was just like a man to do it with a gun. A
fat chance I had of laying my hands on a gun. And even if I
did, I wouldn't have a clue as to what part of me to shoot at."
Ineffective as Cal appears to Esther, she grants that as a male
he has more nerve, more knowhow, and better circumstances
than hers for committing a decisive act. Her attempt at hang-

ing is another failure, and she despairs at her inability to make a good knot. Her most nearly successful suicide attempt is carried out with sleeping pills, the easiest and most passive of the methods, offering a transition through sleep to death, an extension of her earlier retreats into sleep.

In Plath's poetry the urge to die is often given dignity and artistic significance as it is made a kind of awful quest for purity. But there is no grandeur associated with Esther Greenwood's death wish. The tone throughout *The Bell Jar* is grimly humorous, with little pathos developed for the heroine, who is clumsy, unheroic, we could even say shoddy, in her attempts to die. In this coldly realistic and truly ugly version of the suicidal, Plath dispels any romantic notions of the subject we might have had. And such a treatment appropriately reflects Esther's spiteful and unimaginative way of dealing with her own talents: if the world is so heedless of her abilities that the best it can offer her is a job in the fashion industry, she who is one of society's best female products will commit the ultimate offense by stuffing her body into a crevice and leaving it there to die. We cannot admire her method of attack. But neither can we dismiss her as merely one individually neurotic woman who cannot deal with her problems. The issue of Esther's response to her situation aside, the problem she inherits is a thoroughly dismal view of the expectations for a woman in this country, a view which is not uncommon. The waste of her gifts and her life, even though it is not portrayed tragically, is a crucial loss. It brutally raises the question that must be put to Americans: What is a woman to do with her life if she does not follow the conventional pattern of wife and mother? Is there no other valid existence for her?

[Critic] Charles Newman says that *The Bell Jar* gives us "one of the few sympathetic portraits . . . of a girl who refuses to be simply an *event* in anyone's life." It does indeed do this, and it is time such a story was told. Plath presents one of the most unusual and disturbing accounts of a woman ever recorded in American fiction. But no one seems to know where such a story can go or quite what to do with the woman who does not choose to join her life to the lives of others. There is no tradition of women characters dealing with dilemmas that do not revolve around the men or children in their lives. Esther's unconventional pattern can only close off life for her. In her refusal to be like other women she finds no alternative and is trapped in "the bell jar, blank and stopped as a dead baby." The awful irony is that in avoiding one blankness, which for her is a hideously empty view of everything female, Esther takes on another, more terrible and complete. Her brilliance and accomplishments have no power to lead her to a place in the world. Instead, they drive her out of it.

The Bell Jar Is the Story of Sylvia Plath's Mental Breakdown

Linda Wagner-Martin is Hanes Professor of English at the University of North Carolina at Chapel Hill. She has written or edited more than fifty books, including biographies of Zelda Fitzgerald, Gertrude Stein, Ellen Glasgow, and Barbara Kingsolver.

The Bell Jar is the story of a young woman's mental breakdown caused by the unrelenting demands placed on her by the culture of the 1950s and her family, writes Wagner-Martin in the following excerpt. It is a novel of generational conflict—Esther's mother and the other "old ladies" of The Bell Jar are depicted as power-wielding harpies seeking to control her life and smother her personality. The book ends on a note of hope as the destructive old ladies are replaced by Dr. Nolan, who helps guide Esther to mental health.

Ironically, in [Sylvia Plath's mother] Aurelia Plath's own assessment, the crucial event of Sylvia's life was her breakdown and recovery. That her mother never admitted any complicity in that psychological malaise was . . . endemic to her psychology—and, of course, to her daughter's. Mrs. Plath tended to focus on what most readers would think were the externals of the situation: whose car they drove to the outpatient facility, or how Aurelia managed her work schedule to be home most of the time with her daughter. One element of that continuum of details which Mrs. Plath seldom mentions was the existence of what Sylvia saw as frightening electrocon-

Linda Wagner-Martin, *Plath: A Literary Life*. Basingstoke, UK: Macmillan Press, 1999, pp. 33–41. Copyright © 1999 by Linda Wagner-Martin. All rights reserved. Reproduced by permission of Palgrave Macmillan.

vulsive shock treatments—those given during the summer by a psychologist she did not respect, and those given during her rehabilitation at McLean Hospital, this time under the care of Dr. Ruth Buescher, a psychiatrist she did admire and respect— and love.

The entire year that was occupied by her decline into the depression that caused her suicide attempt, and her recovery from that depression, was a time she tried in several ways to erase. There are no journal entries from that year; there are few letters; and there is almost no poetry or fiction. If Plath saw herself as living the life of a writer, existing through the life of the mind and its language, then the period of her breakdown was, in truth, not only a lost year but a death. She subsequently faced the terrifying loss of memory that was bound to accompany shock treatments, but that loss was more easily disguised.

The Perils Women Confront

What could never be disguised was the event—breakdown, suicide attempt, treatment, incarceration in an institution. Society would not forget, nor could society forgive her that indignity. The brilliant and beautiful Sylvia Plath, the Smith scholarship coed whose photograph ran in newspapers across the United States while she was missing during her suicide attempt, was irretrievably moored in the cultural memory of the American 1950s. The question of what would become of that brilliant woman had become a larger cultural question: what man would marry a mad woman? Or as Plath wrote the moving line for Esther Greenwood's boyfriend in *The Bell Jar*, "'I wonder who you'll marry now, Esther . . . I wonder who you'll marry now, Esther. Now you've been,' and Buddy's gesture encompassed the hill, the pines and the severe, snow-gabled buildings breaking up the rolling landscape, 'here.'"

Given all the separable themes that intertwine in Plath's novel, the pervasive one is the autobiography of her breakdown. It is that illness that brings the bell jar down on her, that weakens her grasp on accomplishment and life, and that makes her question the family power that had been so coercive a force in her life choices. *The Bell Jar* shows the ways in which Esther Greenwood is the unquestionable product of her ambitious mother and family, and the ways in which she must deny the influence of those elements before she can come into her own fully defined birth. Esther must reconcile what she wants out of life with the pain she will have to cause her family during her process of attaining her needs. She must stop being the good daughter and become the woman who wants.

An unpleasant book to write, freighted with pain for people she knew loved her deeply, this novel became yet another way to crash through the emotional obstacles that were hedging her in, keeping her from realizing her characteristically wry and often hurtful voice. It is only after Plath finishes writing *The Bell Jar* (she turns the manucript over to its English publishers in November 1961 although the book does not appear until late January 1963) that she comes into the powerful, relentless voice of her last poems.

From its opening scenes, with the recovered Esther Greenwood giving her baby the plastic starfish off the College Board sunglass case, the novel charts what it means to be wife, mother, daughter. Every detail in the novel speaks to some ritualized feminine behavior—whether it be keeping lipsticks in the case they belong in, winning prizes in the New York writing market, daring the eligible Yalie, or finding out with relief that one is not pregnant. From the smallest scenes to the largest, *The Bell Jar* is a tapestry of women's experiences, women's comedy, and all too often, women's tragedy.

It is also a narrative that pays strict attention to what the reader will need to know. Part I sets the novel in the summer of 1953, with the electrocution of the Rosenbergs,[1] an event

---

1. Ethel and Julius Rosenberg were American Communists who were convicted of handing nuclear secrets to the Soviets. They were executed in the electric chair in 1953. The whole affair was controversial and ongoing in the media.

caught in historical time that foreshadows Esther's own electroconvulsive shock treatments later that same summer. Part II lets the reader know that Esther has survived, that she has married and had a child (effectively answering Buddy Willard's interrogation above), and that she has tried to resume a normal existence. As Plath wrote candidly, "I realized we kept piling up these presents because it was as good as free advertising for the firms involved, but I couldn't be cynical. I got such a kick out of all those free gifts showering on to us. For a long time afterward I hid them away, but later, when I was all right again, I brought them out, and I still have them around the house."

In her description of the "Amazon" hotel (the Barbizon [Hotel for Women in New York City]), Plath draws an economic dividing line between the protected and rich young women (going to Katy Gibbs [Secretarial School in New York City] or being secretaries for executives after having gone to Katy Gibbs) who comprise most of the Amazon's residents and the intellectual elite, the College Board women who do not have such clear ambitions to marry well. Esther begins her quasi-nasty monologue, "Girls like that make me sick. I'm so jealous I can't speak." Yet she backtracks to point to the obvious problems with the wealthy playgirl story: "These girls looked awfully bored to me . . . I talked with one of them, and she was bored with yachts and bored with flying around in airplanes and bored with skiing in Switzerland at Christmas and bored with the men in Brazil." The dichotomy between women who have a chance to marry well—and thereby solve all their career problems for the rest of their lives—and those who must make it on their own is forcefully drawn.

Sex Is Central to the Generational Divide

The key narrative in *The Bell Jar*, however, is less economic than it is sexual. If there were ever a point of contention between the generations of Aurelia Plath and her daughter, it was the problem of unmarried women having sex. Nice girls didn't. Pages of women's magazines, basic sex education classes, veiled movies and novels were all devoted to the mandate that women experienced sex only after they married.

Plath's introduction of the other eleven College Board women had to do with their sexuality. Doreen, the Southern woman who was recognizable by her "slightly sweaty smell" in her "dressing gowns the color of skin," was after fun; Betsy, or "Pollyanna Cowgirl" as Doreen called her, was after staying in straight and narrow paths; and invited Esther to do things with her "as if she were trying to save me in some way." The assortment of various episodes that take place in New York are arranged around either pole of sexuality. With Doreen, Esther feels morally superior; with Betsy, she feels corrupt and worldly. Finally, neither woman can serve as a pattern for appropriate behavior, though Esther borrows Betsy's skirt and blouse to wear on the trip back home. The most decisive act she takes toward Doreen is leaving her friend, drunk and sick, to sleep in the hallway after Doreen collapsed at her door.

The way Esther behaves in regard to these friends, and the other college women—as well as toward Jay Cee, the fiction editor, and other magazine personnel—is to become her mother. That disapproving attitude that finds reasons for disliking nearly everyone becomes her trademark; and yet her cynicism leads her into sexual situations she knows would appall her mother. Pretending she must work harder to please Jay Cee, she creates further isolation, when in reality she cannot find a moral balance to use when she interacts with the other college women.

The Old Control the Young

Being unsure is one dilemma, but being angry is another, and different, situation. In *The Bell Jar*, Esther's anger is aimed toward the experienced, successful magazine staff; these women become the objects of her hatred: "Jay Cee wanted to teach me something, all the old ladies I ever knew wanted to teach me something, but I suddenly didn't think they had anything to teach me." For a novel about young women in New York, the fiction spends much of its time dwelling on a bevy of "old ladies." Here is the crux of what Plath defines as a generational mandate: she must listen to older women with money, power, and knowledge because she is dependent on them—for money and knowledge. They pay for her education, they pay for her therapy, they pay for her beauty aides. They instruct her on how to catch a man, how to do well in college, how to write. All these clones of her successful mother, Mrs. Greenwood, who is the epitome of self-satisfied careerism, seem to share an ability to lead non-sexual lives, throwing themselves into their work and their volunteerism (which includes Esther and her mental health) as if they were nuns.

Much of the narrative of *The Bell Jar*, in fact, describes the kind of interaction Esther has with these "old ladies." The initial scene with Jay Cee, when the fiction editor berates Esther for not working hard enough, not knowing enough languages, not trying to learn all there is to know about the fashion magazine world, leads to Esther's memory of the way she has outsmarted her college dean so that she is allowed to take whatever classes she wants, instead of following the schedule for majors. The connection between her memory of getting her way about requirements and her present-time chastizing from Jay Cee is that she knows full well, in retrospect, that she has only hurt herself by changing classes. Pretending to be smarter than authorities, pretending that she knows her own needs, has cost her. The scene with Jay Cee winds down into Esther's hard realization that part of her angst in New York is fueled by her anger at her mother.

The next scene in the novel concerns the writer-mentor who not only funds Esther's college scholarship, but provides advice about the literary world as well. Another memory piece, this episode recounts the way the inexperienced Esther drank the water out of Philomena Guinea's elegant fingerbowl when she had gone to her benefactress's home for lunch. About the voiceless, and victimized, Philomena the reader knows only that she doesn't say a word about Esther's gaffe, but instead tells her only that "she had been very stupid at college."

Esther's Anger at Her Mother Is a Key to Her Psychosis

When Alice Miller says that Plath's *The Bell Jar* was her honest if partially subconscious assessment of the way her psyche had developed, and was developing, in contrast to *Letters Home* which continued the fantasy that she and Aurelia together created, she calls attention to the way art stems from the subconscious as well as the conscious. What does happen in the fusion between conscious and subconscious that writing the novel evoked for Plath is that many of the "old ladies" took on characteristics of her mother. Whereas one might suppose that Philomena Guinea would be more understanding of Esther's writerly talents, in *The Bell Jar* she seems as obtuse—and as set on diminishing her fame and money-making ability—as a Mrs. Greenwood might have been.

Through Mrs. Willard, the mother of her beau Buddy, Esther meets and goes out with Constantin, an interpreter for the UN. In this narrative, Plath can assess notions of romantic love and marriage, but her focus falls more directly on the life of Mrs. Willard, mother of three children, wife of a college teacher, and maker of kitchen rugs. In her choice of the anecdote about Mrs. Willard's devoting hours to weaving a kitchen mat out of strips of her family's clothing, Plath signals her anger about the way society values work. She would have hung the mat on the wall, she says, and viewed it as a piece of art. Instead, Mrs. Willard (only once in the book called "Nelly" and that time by her husband) used it on her floor so that "in a few days it was soiled and dull and indistinguishable from any mat you could buy for under a dollar in the five and ten."

In *The Bell Jar*, Mrs. Willard becomes the voice of society's wisdom about women. It is she who describes a woman's being the place that a man, imaged as an arrow, shoots off from; and it is her son Buddy who explains to Esther that once she has children, she won't want to write poems any longer—that she will understand that poems are dust.

Plath reserves the major part of the novel for the characterization of Mrs. Greenwood, developing it from the perspective of the by-now thoroughly depressed Esther when she arrives home from New York. Even the "motherly" breath of the suburb horrified her, as she noticed that "A summer calm laid its soothing hand over everything, like death." And the first person Esther sees from her bedroom window is the ever-pregnant Dodo Conway, one of the successful debs who had trapped a worthy husband so that she could immediately begin her life work of having children. The plot of matrophobia kicks in earnestly, for Esther must sort through the tangible ramifications of being sexually active, succeeding in the female quest to capture a man, and still being something other than one's mother.

Everything reprehensible about older and asexual women—minor as well as major—comes into play in this section of *The Bell Jar*. Snoring, wearing pincurls "like a row of little bayonets," being dictatorial yet knowing nothing, Mrs. Greenwood is a paragon of generational difference. In some ways, she is also a paragon of parental *in*difference because she clearly does not hear what Esther tells her, nor does she respond to Esther's needs in any meaningful way. What comes from Mrs. Greenwood is a set of platitudes, so commonplace that Esther need not listen to them: "My mother said the cure for thinking too much about yourself was helping somebody who was worse off than you," she noted at the start of her daughter's depression; "We'll act as if all this were a bad dream," she states with some emphasis after Esther's suicide attempt. And the acts that Mrs. Greenwood performs—like getting out an old blackboard and using it to show Esther shorthand symbols—parallel her useless maxims. The most useless, of course, is her dramatic and stubborn reply after Esther has declared that she will have no more shock treatments: her mother then confidently says, "I knew my baby wasn't like that . . . I knew you'd decide to be all right again."

Claiming ownership of Esther (referring to her as "my baby," which, at 19, Esther no longer is) and claiming all knowledge that pertains to her daughter's illness (that her improving is only a matter of will) shows Mrs. Greenwood's true personality. Nothing can jar her complacent belief that she knows all about everything, that she is the perfect mother to a perfect set of children, children whose only responsibility is to present themselves to the world so as to validate their mother's goodness. It is because Esther knows this about her mother that she has decided early in the book, "I would spend the summer writing a novel. That would fix a lot of people."

Coming to terms with some of her more intense motives, Esther sees that anger at her mother is at the root of her illness. She does not need her therapist to explain her anger to her; the first night she spent at home, seeing her mother sleeping in the adjoining twin bed in her room, Esther realized: "My mother turned from a foggy log into a slumbering, middle-aged woman, her mouth slightly open and a snore raveling from her throat. The piggish noise irritated me, and for a while it seemed to me that the only way to stop it would be to take the column of skin and sinew from which it rose and twist it to silence between my hands." No wonder Plath wrote to her brother that this novel was to be published secretly, under a pseudonym, and—as a "pot-boiler." Death wishes about one's mother were not the stuff to satisfy parental dreams.

Whatever comic effect Esther's recognition might have had for the cursory reader, she knew that, if her mother read the book, there was no way of disguising the hatred that motivated such a paragraph. There was no way of explaining away the fact that Esther tried to hang herself with the silk cord of her mother's bathrobe, and that' she stole fifty sleeping pills from her mother's supposedly locked cabinet. Mother and daughter are thereby shown to be complicit in this suicide effort, however innocent of Esther's aims her mother pretends to be. . . .

The masterful change in the last quarter of *The Bell Jar*, a narrative move that takes the novel out of the realm of autobiography—even if comparatively honest autobiography, is that Plath transfers the parental role from Mrs Greenwood to Dr Nolan. By ending Esther's torture in the mental institution by providing her with both an apt physician and a refuge from her mother's frightening control, the novel takes on the aura of promise that Plath was trying to create. Finally, *The Bell Jar* convinces the reader that its author understands the subtleties and the full ranges of mental and physical health.

Contemporary Perspectives on Depression

Both Depression and a Risk Factor for Suicide Run in Families

Paul Fink

Paul Fink is a consultant and psychiatrist in Bala Cynwyd, Pennsylvania, and a professor of psychiatry at Temple University.

The suicide of Sylvia Plath's son Nicholas Hughes, a successful biologist, raises the question of whether or not a tendency toward depression and suicide is inherited, writes Fink in the following viewpoint. Researchers have identified two specific genes that are linked to depression and suicidal behavior. Psychiatrists treating patients with a family history of depression and/or suicide need to be vigilant about other risk factors, which include solitariness, a history of sexual or physical abuse, and expressions of hopelessness, Fink concludes.

The suicide of Nicholas Hughes, the son of the famed poets Sylvia Plath and Ted Hughes, not only has led to much conjecture and age-old questions about heritability of depression. It also raises questions about suicide, suicide clusters, and the mimicking of suicidal behavior in families.

Depression Can Lead to Suicide

Nicholas Hughes was a well-known citizen of Fairbanks, Alaska, an acknowledged scholar in his own field of biology, and he clearly eschewed discussions about his mother, according to *The New York Times* [in "A New Chapter of Grief in Plath-Hughes Legacy," April 11, 2009].

Paul Fink, "Fink! Still at Large: A Recent Suicide Raises Questions About the Heritability of Depression and Suicidal Behavior. What Should We Be Looking for While Working with Depressed Patients?" *Clinical Psychiatry News*, May 2009, p. 26. Copyright © 2009 by Paul Fink. All rights reserved. Reproduced by permission.

We are frequently confronted by a suicide in which the victim is described as being in good shape with, ostensibly, "everything to live for." What goes on in the mind of someone whose career is going well, who is in a good intimate relationship, and who has a supportive social circle—and who nonetheless chooses to end his or her life? It is very mysterious.

Yet it appears that despite appearances, such people are extremely vulnerable to minor stressors—a word, a small event, an attack on their self-esteem—and much more so than is the average person.

According to the piece in *The Times*, Nicholas Hughes had battled depression for years, "as his mother had, and on a recent trip to New Zealand he had even talked of suicide."

The average person rarely, if ever, expresses this kind of vulnerability—the feeling of having been hurt, attacked, undermined, or betrayed. But people with depression frequently have these feelings. And these feelings and concomitant mood swings can lead to suicide.

Having a Relative Commit Suicide Increases Risk

What did his mother's suicide and the suicide deaths of several other important people in his life contribute to his ending his own life? Although most Americans are familiar with suicide as a possible method for exit, it is not something most people think about very often or even consider as an option.

However, people with suicide in their lives are more likely to think about it and might even consider suicide normal behavior. One of the criteria in measuring lethality when someone expresses a suicidal wish is whether a significant family member—particularly first-degree relatives—has committed suicide.

According to the American Psychiatric Association's [APA's] *Practice Guidelines for the Assessment of Patients With Suicidal Behaviors*, other factors associated with an increased risk for suicide include recent lack of social support (including living alone); sexual and physical abuse; hopelessness; thought constriction (tunnel vision); male gender; white race; and widowed, divorced, or single marital status, particularly for men.

There is growing literature demonstrating that depression and suicide have a genetic basis. For example, a few years ago, researchers in Germany found that two genes might be involved in the vulnerability for suicidality: intronic polymorphisms of the tryptophan hydroxylase 1 (TPH 1) gene, and the insertion/deletion polymorphism of the serotonin transporter gene (5-HTTLPR).

As researchers continue to look for diagnostic specific genes, we see suggestions of such heritability in family histories as we examine and evaluate patients.

We often find that a parent or grandparent has suffered from depression, and the patient will say, "I've been depressed all my life," with little recognition of stressors that have pushed them further and further into a depressive state. Such patients often have thought about suicide and/or made attempts. We always worry about patients who have thought about it or tried it. The patient might succeed in ending his or her life. What should we do?

Many Suicides Feel Worthless

The story of Mr. Hughes sounds atypical. From the outside, it looked as if he was having a good day. He told his companion that he was going out for a walk, but he actually carried out his suicide instead. His friends knew him as a man of "immense energy and curiosity" who pursued his scientific career and received a lot of professional recognition and positive feedback. These are not the ingredients that usually lead a person to commit suicide. Suicidal intent makes more psychological sense in cases in which observers can detect a deep sense of worthlessness and reported failures or disappointments in one's career.

I interviewed a patient recently who had just tried to kill himself for the fourth time. He told me that every night as a child he would receive a severe beating and was told that he was worthless—repeatedly. He internalized this message and quit his most recent job when his boss wanted to promote him to a supervisory position. He said he quit because he felt he couldn't do the job. Therefore, the message started early and was deeply ingrained in him.

This is markedly different from what we know about Nicholas Hughes, whose father reportedly advised him when he was still a boy to "let his mother go." This is a rare message from a father to a son, but his father clearly recognized how poisonous his mother's fame and suicide might be.

Another important factor to consider is the problem of the cluster phenomenon in suicide. It sometimes resembles a biologic infection in which suicide spreads via contact. There have been cases of a high school student's suicide resulting in copycat behavior by classmates. In such cases, it appears that the suicide copier might have already contemplated suicide, and the successful suicide of a friend or acquaintance gave them the courage to proceed.

Sylvia Plath's death did not go unnoticed in her son's mind, and he might well have seen this as a way to "end it all." This cliche is also well-known. We hear people expressing their desire to stop the pressure they feel and to do so in a way that is quick, efficient, and final.

One of the noticeable facts mentioned in the *New York Times* article is the repeated concern expressed by his friends about his privacy—not to intrude after his death or his memorial services with too much "investigation" about his life. That respect for a person's privacy can be isolating.

People prone to depression can misinterpret such helpfulness and feel they are responsible for people avoiding others. We can only speculate on the significance this emphasis on privacy might have had in his suicide. Even though Mr.

The Hemingway family in 1918. Several members of the Hemingway family committed suicide, including the novelist Ernest Hemingway (third from the left), his father, and two of his siblings. The death of Ernest Hemingway's granddaughter Margaux was also ruled a suicide. © Reuters/Landov.

Hughes was well-regarded and even loved by his family and friends, he seemed to guard his privacy carefully.

A Support System Is Important in Preventing Suicide

One cannot really talk about suicide without a deep understanding of depression, which Mr. Hughes seems to have fought all his life. But one of his friends told *The Times* that he shared the Alaskan "reverence for being alone," which can be very devastating for a depressive. Nothing is more important than a support system for [a] person who is subject to mood changes and who can hurt himself with negative ideas.

In my practice, I check out a patient's support system—whom do they call, depend upon, and feel close to? Many patients become very dependent on the psychiatrist or therapist, who is the only person they trust. Other protective factors, ac-

133

cording to the APA practice guidelines, include children in the home (except among people with mood disorder or postpartum psychosis), pregnancy, religiosity, and life satisfaction.

The Times piece said that Mr. Hughes' colleagues "knew of his struggle with depression," but they also said he worked hard to manage it. Still, in September 2006, his bosses grew alarmed when he did not show up for work for several days. Eventually, the state police were asked to check up on him.

It is clear that despite the concern of people around him—people who knew of his depression and worried that he might kill himself—he was still successful in ending his life. The article describes a specific stressor in Nicholas Hughes' life—discord between his sister and their stepmother. So although one can collect clues and factors that contribute to a person committing suicide, it can never known for certain what occurred to propel a person to do carry it out.

The critical psychological factors in depression are helplessness, hopelessness, worthlessness, and guilt. We don't know of the presence of the first three in Mr. Hughes, but guilt is an important, often pervasive factor.

I have a cousin whose mother died of breast cancer when he was 14 years old. He is in his early 50s now and has irrationally blamed himself for her death throughout his entire life.

His mother was in a great deal of physical and psychological pain, and pushed her children away from her at the end of her life. Such secret pain is common, and who knows what hidden effect Ms. Plath's suicide might have had on her son? We do know that the unconscious mind is a deep reservoir for this kind of irrational perception. He didn't like to talk about his mother or father, but the significance of this fact, and the possible guilt he felt over his mother's suicide will remain forever unknown.

As we psychiatrists work with depressed people, looking for unconscious guilt is vital, and the only way to address this guilt is to force and foster discussions of these factors in their therapy.

In the case of the family member mentioned earlier, his hatred for his heroin-addicted mother who physically and emotionally abused him every night has to be very intense. To prevent his successful suicide, we need to get him to recognize his hatred for her cruelty and neglect and to find it acceptable—not a cause of guilt.

I have tried to give an overview of the factors contributing to multiple suicides in families, and the role of depression in heritability of suicide. We must reflect on the many unanswered questions when we read about the sons of famous poets killing themselves. It's our job and our duty to think these questions through, because we all encounter similar situations all too often in our professional lives.

Perfectionism in Gifted Teenagers Can Be Deadly

Laurie Hyatt

Laurie Hyatt is an assistant professor in the Psychology Department at Barton College.

Gifted adolescents have special needs that, if not met, can result in suicide, claims Hyatt in the following viewpoint. In her case study of a gifted young woman who killed herself at age eighteen, Hyatt found four factors that contributed to the suicide: being bullied and rejected at school, the influence of peers, perfectionism, and lack of trust of adults. She recommends four steps to reduce the risk of suicide among gifted teens. First, parents and teachers need to reduce bullying. Second, teachers and parents need to establish deeper bonds with students. Third, parents and teachers need to become more aware of the special needs of gifted children. Fourth, children need to learn they do not have to be perfect.

This article describes a case study of a gifted adolescent female who took her life at age 18 using a firearm. The personal, environmental, and cultural variables that may have contributed to her suicide were examined through interviews of family members, original documents, and other artifacts, including a videotape that was a compilation of events throughout the subject's life. The purpose of this psychological autopsy was to determine what factors led her to end her pain by choosing death over life. . . .

The subject of this study was nominated by her mother in response to the Internet solicitation. Amber (pseudonym), had

Laurie Hyatt, "A Case Study of a Gifted Female Adolescent: Implications for Prediction and Prevention," *Journal for the Education of the Gifted*, Summer 2010, pp. 512–35. Copyright © 2010 by Laurie Hyatt. All rights reserved. Reproduced by permission of SAGE Publications, Inc.

taken her life 10 years before, when she was 18 years of age. Amber had an IQ of 140 and had scored in the 98th and 99th percentiles in the math and language portions of the Iowa Tests of Basic Skills taken in second grade. She was served by gifted classes in school, was a member of MENSA [an organization for people with high IQs], and was recognized as "Most Intelligent" by her high school senior classmates. Amber was also a prolific writer of poetry and prose and the parents had kept the writings, which would be made available to me. . . .

Findings from This Study

Findings from this study focused on Amber's individual characteristics; her family, school, and extracurricular experiences; and her cultural influences. For the purpose of this article, however, with the emphasis on the relevance to education, I will delineate only four findings in particular. First, Amber's frustration, anger, and unhappiness seemed, at least in part, to be directly related to her experiences of being bullied, rejected, and misunderstood at school. In addition, I discovered that Amber had contemplated suicide for 7 years prior to her death and had colluded with school peers about possible methods of taking her life. For example, she wrote that a peer gave her instructions [on how] to blow up her car. Another peer suggested jumping in front of a train after ingesting pills and liquor. Another wanted to complete suicide with her. . . . Third, Amber's perfectionism contributed to an inability to see her life as having value. Her mother shared many specific examples of Amber's aspirations to be the best, such as her plan to be the class valedictorian. Amber also wrote of her feelings of failure when she did not become valedictorian. Finally, Amber very specifically, through her words and through her actions, expressed a lack of trust and a resistance to communication with adults who might have been helpful to her. These main points will be discussed in more detail in the following pages.

Being Bullied, Rejected, and Misunderstood

Amber was bullied, rejected, and misunderstood by peers, teachers, and administrators. Even in kindergarten, Amber was called names by her peers. "I remember in kindergarten she came home crying that the other children called her ugly," her mother related. She was obviously not ugly and her mother tried to explain to her that they were just trying to bother her and to ignore them. Since Amber's suicide, her mother has worried that she inadvertently gave her daughter the message not to confide her feelings.

In addition to feeling rejected by the children who were bullying her at school, Amber also felt misunderstood by teachers. In the second grade, her teacher called Amber's mother to complain that Amber was misbehaving in class by being restless and wearing her sunglasses during a standardized test session. After some discussion of her concerns, the teacher admitted that she did not know anything about giftedness and that perhaps Amber was bored in class rather than purposefully being difficult and oppositional. . . .

Suicidal Ideation and Collaborating with Peers

Shortly before her suicide, Amber wrote about specific "Reasons to Leave," "Reasons to Stay," and "Plans." In a list of 23 Reasons to Leave, she included "I've strongly considered it since 5th GRADE!!! I'm obviously serious." I was not able to identify any particular stressor that occurred in the fifth grade or before that would have caused her to contemplate suicide at such a young age. She was, after all, still in elementary school. An accumulation of many factors apparently led to her feelings of hopelessness and unhappiness. In the fifth grade, she wrote a mixture of poetry and prose in a spiral notebook. She wrote of fears of her mother getting hurt, yearnings to be rich and famous, worries about people who were hungry and her desire to help them, frequent insomnia, and, yes, she indirectly wrote about death. Her alluding to death was in poems and prose in which she personified a tree as if it was herself and wrote of what would happen if it died. She seemed to also have a concern, here again, masked by using third person in her writing, that she was insane and would die of that insanity. So, as early as age 10, she thought that she was so different that she might be unstable and that instability might prove to be lethal. Amber wrote of cutting her wrist when she was 11 years old, but did not carry out this plan because her mother came home. In a freshman high school honors English assignment, which Amber titled, "Suicide," she wrote of her desire to take her life. The teacher put a big red check by it, indicating that she was getting credit for completing the assignment, but obviously the teacher did not really read the content. Amber's pattern of behavior at school also changed overtly in her junior and senior years. She showed anger at the school librarian. She walked out of class a couple of times. She went along with classmates who wanted to change a video being shown by a substitute teacher who had a habit of showing a video and leaving for the rest of the class period. This was a significant behavior change from previous years.

Many adolescents knew of Amber's plans, but no one confided their concerns to an adult or even to a peer who would get help. One student shared her knowledge of a previous suicide attempt by Amber with Amber's mother a week after her suicide. "Why didn't you tell me?" her mother asked. The friend's response was that when Amber did not go through with it, she thought that Amber was not serious. This may indicate a need to educate young people about the importance of sharing their knowledge of another's suicidal ideation or suicide attempts with those who can be helpful in preventing the suicide. Two other pieces of evidence indicate that Amber had included others in discussions about suicide. She received a letter from a male friend, which was found by Amber's mother after her death, in which suicide was discussed. In her list of "Reasons to Leave," "Reasons to Stay," and "Plans," under "Plans" she listed three ways that she had considered taking her life, two of which involved specifically named people. These findings are similar to the findings of previous psychological autopsies in which suicide was discussed among peers as a "viable and honorable solution" [as quoted in a 1996 article by researcher T.L. Cross and others].

Perfectionism Is Unrealistic

In her [2004] study on perfectionism, Speirs Neumeister concluded that not only do parents, teachers, and peers influence young people to feel as if they have to be perfect, but this can also be a self-determined drive. She categorized perfection into two types, socially prescribed and self-oriented. The author prefaced her research study with a personal example of her own perfectionism that she could only attribute to her own personality, not to any pressure from outside. The destructive effects of perfectionism have been studied by many researchers. Although striving for perfection would seem an admirable trait, for gifted adolescents perceived failure can lead to guilt, depression, anxiety, and even suicide. Many gifted adolescents do not give themselves permission to be less than perfect. Their emotional need to be perfect is, of course, unrealistic. When the [musical] prodigy Brandenn Bremmer was asked about his giftedness in an interview with Alissa Quart in 2004, less than a year before taking his life at age 14, he responded, "America is a society that demands perfection." Quart noted [in 2006] that "it was interesting that I had asked him about giftedness, but the word perfection was foremost in his mind." . . .

Amber's high expectations for herself are reflected in her writings about her disappointments about not achieving the honor of class valedictorian, not being accepted by Harvard or Princeton, and not having enough friends. Even though she was accepted to a university with a very good reputation, she wrote that one "Reason to Leave" was "Won't go to a good college." Amber's mother stated that when she did not achieve the status of valedictorian, an aspiration that she had since eighth grade, she gave up. She had to be the best or life was not worth living, in her estimation.

Lack of Trust in Adults

Amber's perception was that adults could not be trusted. She refused to go to a counselor when her mother suggested it after a breakup with a boyfriend. Amber retorted that she could talk to her friends about her problems and that the counselor would focus on what was wrong with her. As Amber expressed in the "Inculcations" poem, she perceived teachers as being rigid authoritarians. She felt that she would not be heard. She also wrote of "Conformity" and felt that adults want young people to conform to their ways and are not open to new ideas. In other words, adults do not listen. She did not confide her thoughts of taking her life to her parents or to any adults. Amber and her mother often disagreed about topics ranging from school teachers to relationships. Once, after becoming angry during an argument, Amber declared that she would not confide again—and she did not.

Amber's Case Is Not Uncommon

This case study raises many questions about the dynamics that influence young people to take their lives and, hopefully, adds to the urgency of the need for further research regarding suicide among gifted adolescents. Some of the factors that seem to have influenced Amber to take her life were also experienced by adolescents who were studied in other psychological autopsies. Four of the contributing factors discovered in this article were being bullied, the influences of peers, perfectionism, and a lack of trust in others.

Amber was bullied beginning in kindergarten and came home crying from school. In addition to complaining to her mother about the hurtful remarks of schoolmates, she also wrote about the hurt that she experienced from the negative remarks of others. How much influence did being bullied have on her decision to take her life? Apparently a great deal because she wrote that two of her "Reasons to Leave" were "Fear of further rejection" and "Unbearable loneliness."

How much were Amber's plans to take her life influenced by others? The influences of peers were reflected in a letter from a male friend who suggested suicide to Amber. In addition, under "Plans" in her writings she stated, "Something with Shawn," and "Blow up car via Danny's instructions." Also, her third plan to place herself in "Front of train and lots of pills and liquor" was referenced in other prose as being an idea of a peer.

Amber's perfectionism seemed to be a third contributor to her choice to die. She wrote in "Reasons to Leave," that "I'm on top now and can only descend" and "Won't go to a good college." She added that she felt rejected when she was not valedictorian and irrationally stated "I accomplish nothing." Her high aspirations were shared when she wrote in a piece titled "If I Could Be Anyone for a Day," that "Harvard and Yale would both build statues and dedicate them to me. They would read: This statue is dedicated to the rich, famous, and beautiful lawyer . . . who got her doctorate here."

Amber wrote that she had contemplated suicide since the fifth grade in her "Reasons to Leave" column. How could she have suffered in silence and not confided in adults while writing of her struggles in her numerous poems, prose, and journals? The findings of other psychological autopsies of gifted youth are similar. Although the adolescents in those studies wrote introspectively about their difficulties and even obsessed about their troubles, they confided in other adolescents, but not in adults. Amber's parents did not know that she was thinking of taking her life. . . . Lack of trust in adults was expressed by Amber to her mother when she refused counseling, saying that a counselor would just find something wrong with her and that she would, instead, talk with her friends. She also did not trust teachers and administrators in the school system. She was furious when she was not allowed to make up school work after missing some days at school. Up until that point she was in line to be the valedictorian. She expressed frustration with teachers in her poem "Inculcations," . . . in which she berated adults for thinking that they are always right. A librarian was the target of Amber's anger when she was restricted from reading some books due to her age and grade in school. Amber confided in her best friend that she was contemplating suicide but did not share her plans with an adult who would have provided guidance. . . .

Steps to Prevent Suicide

Findings from this study can serve as catalysts for the following actions:

1. Reduce bullying. Effective education for students, teachers, and parents regarding the destructive effects of bullying and preventative measures is needed. This could be done through mandatory character education training beginning in kindergarten. Teaching empathy can be incorporated into the class curricula. . . .

2. Create personal connections between adolescents and adults. Establishing relationships of trust between students and teachers, counselors, and administrators requires time spent together individually as well as in classes and groups. With smaller classes of under 20 students, teachers can be more aware of individual needs and issues. Counselors should meet with each student individually two times per year, not because there is a problem, but because they wish to establish trusting relationships. Education should include a change in the role of counselor from the person who diagnoses pa-

thologies, solves problems, or worse yet, disciplines, to a guide who can be helpful and is available to every student. . . .

3. Educate parents, teachers, and administrators on the characteristics and social and emotional issues of gifted adolescents. Parents, teachers, administrators, and gifted students themselves would benefit from classes or workshops in which the characteristics of gifted children and adolescents are taught. Knowing what to expect as a result of being gifted helps to identify what behaviors might be attributed to giftedness and what behaviors might be attributed to depression or feelings of worthlessness. Also, what are the vulnerabilities associated with being gifted? An example would be the likelihood that gifted children and adolescents will be made fun of and isolated just because they are different. . . .

4. Teach adolescents that self-worth is not dependent on being perfect. As implied earlier in this article, Brandenn Bremmer was aware that his own perfectionism stemmed from societal messages. Post messages on school walls and websites emphasizing the fact that no one can be the best at everything and that success is not defined by perfection.

In conclusion, preventing suicide among gifted adolescents is contingent on establishing meaningful relationships at home and at school, creating an atmosphere of emotional safety and trust at school, incorporating the teaching of empathy into school curricula, and teaching young people that self-worth is defined by uniqueness rather than perfection. Realizing that a child's perceptions are molded by the culture in which he or she lives, we must scrutinize the cultural messages that young people are internalizing and acting upon. How can we recreate the school environment so that children feel valued and safe? How can we shift the cultural messages on television and the

Internet from an emphasis on perfection to an emphasis on uniqueness? How can close, trusting relationships be established between adults and adolescents so that young people seek out adults for guidance? When we as a society have taken constructive action on these issues, then a firm foundation will be developed on which talented and creative souls like Amber can flourish.

Unrealistic Pressures and a Lack of Societal Safeguards Cause Depression in Teenage Girls

Maxine Frith

Maxine Frith is a social affairs correspondent for the Independent, *a British national morning newspaper published in London.*

Teenage girls of the twenty-first century are at greater risk than ever before of depression, other mental illnesses, and even suicide, Frith claims in the following viewpoint. She reports that contributing factors such as pressure at school, society's obsession with physical perfection, and family problems are compounded by an increased access to drugs and alcohol. Engaging in risky behavior as a response to stress, as they see the adults around them do, only adds to their problems.

Girls as young as 14 now suffer from depression, are debilitated by hatred of their own bodies or feel unable to cope with the pressures of life.

A survey has found that one in 10 teenage girls describes herself as an "emotional wreck", while 60 per cent feel insecure and more than half say they are plagued by self-doubt.

The survey of 2,000 girls with an average age of 14 for the teen magazine Bliss found that more than a third currently feel "unhappy and miserable".

Mental health specialists warned that girls as young as 14 are copying the binge-drinking and stressed-out behaviour of

Maxine Frith, "Teenage Girls 'Depressed by Modern Life'," *Independent*, February 24, 2005. www.independent.co.uk. Reproduced by permission.

adults around them as they try to cope with the stresses of modern life. They said that family breakdown, bullying at school and society's obsession with the "perfect body" were fuelling the lack of confidence among pubescent girls.

More than a third questioned live with a single parent or in a step family. Four out of 10 said they regularly felt depressed about life, while six per cent did not feel life was worth living.

Two thirds complained about the heavy pressure to achieve academically, while more than half said family problems had taken a toll on their emotional health. And two thirds said they had been bullied at some point in their lives.

Why Are So Many Teenage Girls Depressed?

Lisa Smosarski, the editor of Bliss, said: "We live in a rough, tough world and there are no society safeguards any more to protect young people. They have gradually been eroded over the years, and even the few remaining ones are being ripped down. Cannabis has been downgraded and 24-hours-a-day drinking is on the horizon. It's a free for all, but young people need boundaries to feel secure."

She added: "Teenage girls are expected to cope with a cocktail of broken homes, endless school work, emotional pressures and the availability of drink and drugs. It is a cocktail that is seriously damaging the psyche of teenage girls."

Health specialists are concerned that the toll on the mental, physical and emotional health of teenage girls is being fuelled by worrying increases in their use of alcohol, cigarettes and drugs. The number of girls under 14 who are hospitalised with mental health problems triggered by alcohol has risen by 25 per cent over the past seven years, according to a study in the British Medical Journal.

Maxine Frith reports that in the twenty-first century, teenage girls are especially vulnerable to depression. © Picture Partners/Alamy.

Teenage girls in Britain drink more than their male peers, with reports that some are developing serious alcohol-related liver problems before they reach their 16th birthdays.

The survey found that a third of 14-year-old girls are already drinking alcohol every week, while one in five has tried drugs. Four out of ten said drink and drugs are too readily available.

Tina Radziszewicz, a psychotherapist, said: "We live in a society where adults deal with the stresses of modern life by misusing alcohol and drugs and jumping from one sexual partner to another. Sadly, young people are copying what they see around them.

"This risky behaviour brings a whole new set of problems to teenage girls already struggling with worries about their exams, parents' relationships, boyfriends, bullying and the pressure to look perfect."

She went on: "Rather than blaming teenagers, everyone from parents to the Government needs to wake up to the fact that the emotional and mental health of our young people is in crisis."

Pressures of Adolescence

Anna Ross will turn 14 next month. She lives with her mother, stepfather, brother and sister in Sawbridgeworth, Hertfordshire, and attends a local co-ed private school.

"I do feel really pressured, especially at school," she said. "We have a lot of homework and classes and it does really worry me. I keep having things go round and round my head and it can be difficult to cope with."

According to Anna, most girls her age are under constant pressure from both each other and magazines and other media to stay slim.

"You have to look perfect and be perfect if you don't want to get picked on at school and that is really hard to achieve," she said.

Peer Pressure and Bullying

"When we were younger it was just a bit of pushing around but now there is a lot of name calling and talking behind your back and it can be really difficult to know how to deal with that. There is a lot of bullying, especially at school."

Girls in her peer group are already harming themselves and turning to drink to cope with their problems, Anna said. She added: "A lot of people my age do feel miserable and depressed about all the pressures they have got on them.

"Sometimes I feel okay but other times it really does just keep building up. I feel happy at home most of the time but things can get me down."

Hard Questions to Ask After a Cry for Help

Perri Klass

Perri Klass, a pediatrician, is a professor of journalism and pediatrics at New York University and medical director of Reach Out and Read, a national literacy organization. She is the author of several works of fiction and nonfiction, including Treatment Kind and Fair: Letters to a Young Doctor.

Getting to the root of what is troubling teenagers is not easy, suggests Klass in the following viewpoint. Many adolescents, especially boys, will not admit to being depressed or sad. It is easier for most teens to admit to being stressed out. It is important for pediatricians and psychiatrists to ask questions that elicit the truth so that at-risk youth can be helped and suicide prevented.

Some time ago I got an e-mail message from one of my students: She couldn't come to class. She was having terrible problems, her life had fallen apart, she was just sitting and crying. She was sorry, but her assignment would be late.

Talking About Suicide Is Hard

Immediately, my mind went back to a familiar acronym: Headsss. The letters stand for an interviewing technique developed in 1991 for adolescent patients—H for home (the doctor starts by asking about the teenager's home situation), E for education and employment, A for activities. And then, in a progression meant to move from less sensitive topics to touchier subjects, it is on to D for drugs and finally the three S's: sexuality, suicide and safety.

Perri Klass, MD, "Hard Questions to Ask After a Cry for Help," *New York Times*, December 8, 2009. Copyright © 2009 by The New York Times. All rights reserved. Reprinted with permission.

These are not easy questions to ask—even home and education may be fraught subjects for many adolescents. Sometimes a teenager will say, "If I tell you something, will you absolutely promise to keep it a secret?"

And the pediatrician must respond with the truth—or, much better, establish the rules with every patient, before the question even comes up. "I say this in front of the parent and the teen," Dr. Michelle S. Barratt, a professor of pediatrics at the University of Texas Medical School at Houston, told me. "'I'm going to talk to your teen about some things that are easier to talk about without a parent in the room, and I'm going to keep things confidential unless it's life-threatening.' And I use those words."

No, these aren't easy conversations. "There's been a fear that talking to children or adolescents about suicide is somehow suggestive or puts them at higher risk," said Dr. Benjamin N. Shain, head of child and adolescent psychiatry at NorthShore University HealthSystem outside Chicago. "Repeated studies have shown this is not the case."

Dr. Shain was the lead author of the American Academy of Pediatrics' 2007 statement on suicide and suicide attempts in adolescents. As a psychiatrist, he has experience treating adolescents who have attempted suicide, and he is a strong advocate for screening in primary care settings.

In fact, asking the question does not awaken thoughts of suicide—suicidal ideation, as we call it. A 2005 study in *The Journal of the American Medical Association* looked at more than 2,000 New York State high school students in a randomized controlled trial; those screened were not more likely to report suicidal thoughts in the following days.

Stress Can Be a Better Indicator than Depression

Dr. Kenneth R. Ginsburg, an adolescent medicine specialist at the Children's Hospital of Philadelphia and the author of "A

Parent's Guide to Building Resilience in Children and Teens," would prefer to think in terms of a different mnemonic: Sshadess. That first S reminds you to start the conversation by asking about the teenager's strengths—about what is going well in your patient's life—and move from there to school, home and activities before approaching drugs.

And before you get to the S's, there is the E for emotion, which, Dr. Ginsburg said, should be much more than screening for depression. "If you start by asking boys if they're depressed or sad, most boys will deny that," he told me. "If you start by saying, 'So, are you stressed out?'—every boy, no matter how big and strong, every girl, no matter how much she wants to portray herself as being in control, will admit to stress."

Markers for depression may help identify adults at risk for suicide, but they are not a reliable way to screen adolescents. "Only about half of kids who kill themselves are depressed in the way that we think about depression—sad, not taking care of themselves, not sleeping or sleeping too much, not eating or eating too much," Dr. Ginsburg said. The other half may be impulsive, angry, disappointed, trying to get even.

Dr. Shain said adolescents often changed their ideas and their plans. So an assessment has to go beyond the feelings of the moment to include thoughts they have had, dangerous ways they have behaved and the important questions of intent and ambivalence.

"Sometimes you'll get an 'I don't know' answer," he explained, "which might be ominous, might mean they don't know or might mean they don't want to tell you."

If a teenager does acknowledge thinking about suicide, there are many more questions to be asked. Dr. Lydia A. Shrier, director of clinic-based research on adolescent and young-adult medicine at Children's Hospital Boston, said some young people chronically struggled with these issues.

"If I responded every time they said, 'Yes, I have these thoughts,' by sending them to the E.R. [emergency room], they would spend their lives there," Dr. Shrier said. "You have to ask, but then you have to get the rich detail of somebody's internal experience."

The point of asking, after all, is to help. That means helping in a crisis, of course. "I tell patients, 'If you tell me that you want to kill yourself and you can't tell somebody when you have those feelings and you can't make a safety plan with me, then I can't let you leave this office,'" Dr. Shrier said. But it also means finding therapeutic resources for those who are struggling and helping them understand they are entitled to feel better.

"Kids don't want it to be ignored," Dr. Ginsburg said. "It's a cry for help. No one wants to know that their cry for help was ignored.

"They might act angry. But what you're communicating is: 'I really listened, I heard you. I'm going to see that you get help, I'm going to take the action you deserve.'"

I e-mailed back to my student, "Please come to class." And when she did, I asked her how she was doing. She replied that she was seriously stressed.

I wanted to do a full Headsss assessment. But I was her teacher, not her doctor. So I suggested, as delicately as I could, that with all the stress in her life, she might want to go to student health services, where counseling was available. I walked her over, to make sure she got there.

For Further Discussion

1. In Chapter 1, Dorothea Krook writes about Sylvia Plath's struggle for normalcy. She describes how she appeared on the surface to be a happily married wife and mother while struggling with depression. What are some of the events she relates in Plath's last year that could have pushed her over the edge into depression and suicide?

2. In Chapter 2, Gordon Lameyer writes that Plath uses the literary technique of doubles to represent the conflicts Esther Greenwood is experiencing. What are some of the negative images Plath presents, and what do they represent? What are some of the positive images?

3. In Chapter 2, Mason Harris writes of *The Bell Jar*, "Nowhere have I found so forceful a depiction of what it was like to be an adolescent in the stifling, hermetically-sealed world of the Eisenhower 'Fifties." In what ways is the culture Plath describes different from the culture of today? In what ways is it similar?

For Further Reading

Kate Chopin, *The Awakening*. Chicago: Herbert S. Stone, 1899.

Michael Cunningham, *The Hours*. New York: Farrar, Straus & Giroux, 1998.

Jeffrey Eugenides, *The Virgin Suicides*. New York: Farrar, Straus & Giroux, 1993.

F. Scott Fitzgerald, *Tender Is the Night*. New York: Charles Scribner's Sons, 1934.

Janet Frame, *Faces in the Water*. New York: Braziller, 1961.

Joanne Greenberg, *I Never Promised You a Rose Garden*. New York: Holt, Rinehart and Winston, 1964.

Susanna Kaysen, *Girl, Interrupted*. New York: Turtle Bay Books, 1993.

Ken Kesey, *One Flew over the Cuckoo's Nest*. New York: Viking Press, 1962.

Wally Lamb, *She's Come Undone*. New York: Pocket Books, 1992.

John Neufeld, *Lisa, Bright and Dark*. New York: S.G. Phillips, 1969.

Jodi Picoult, *The Pact*. New York: Morrow, 1998.

Sylvia Plath, *Ariel*. London: Faber and Faber, 1965.

Sylvia Plath, *The Collected Poems*. Cutchogue, NY: Buccaneer Books, 1981.

J.D. Salinger, *The Catcher in the Rye*. Boston: Little, Brown, 1951.

Virginia Woolf, *Mrs. Dalloway*. London: Hogarth Press, 1947.

Bibliography

Books

Eileen M. Aird — *Sylvia Plath.* New York: Barnes & Noble, 1973.

Paul Alexander — *Rough Magic: A Biography of Sylvia Plath.* New York: Viking, 1991.

Therese J. Borchard — *Beyond Blue: Surviving Depression and Anxiety and Making the Most of Bad Genes.* New York: Center Street, 2009.

Edward Butscher — *Sylvia Plath: Method and Madness.* New York: Seabury, 1975.

Katy Sara Culling — *Screaming in Silence: Suicide, Attempted Suicide and Self-Harm Recovery.* London: Chipmunkapublishing, 2010.

Deborah S. Gentry — *Suicide in the Works of Kate Chopin and Sylvia Plath.* New York: Peter Lang, 2006.

Ronald Hayman — *The Death and Life of Sylvia Plath.* London: Heinemann, 1991.

Pat MacPherson — *Reflecting on "The Bell Jar."* New York: Routledge, 1991.

Janet Malcolm — *The Silent Woman: Sylvia Plath and Ted Hughes.* New York: Knopf, 1994.

Jacqueline Rose   *The Haunting of Sylvia Plath.*
                    London: Virago, 1991.

Anne Stevenson   *Bitter Fame: A Life of Sylvia Plath.*
                    Boston: Houghton Mifflin, 1989.

Linda   *"The Bell Jar": A Novel of the Fifties.*
Wagner-Martin   New York: Twayne, 1992.

Linda   *Sylvia Plath: The Critical Heritage.*
Wagner-Martin   London: Routledge & Kegan Paul,
                    1988.

Periodicals

Kate A. Baldwin   "The Radical Imaginary of *The Bell
                    Jar*," *Novel: A Forum on Fiction*, Fall
                    2004.

Marilyn Boyer   "The Disabled Female Body as a
                    Metaphor for Language in Sylvia
                    Plath's *The Bell Jar*," *Women's Studies:
                    An Interdisciplinary Journal*,
                    March–April 2004.

E. Miller Budick   "The Feminist Discourse of Sylvia
                    Plath's *The Bell Jar*," *College English*,
                    vol. 49, no. 8, 1987.

Lauren Collins   "Friend Game," *New Yorker*, January
                    21, 2008.

Brian Cooper   "Sylvia Plath and the Depression
                    Continuum," *Journal of the Royal
                    Society of Medicine*, June 2003.

Teresa De   "Rebirth in *The Bell Jar*," *Women's
Lauretis   Studies*, vol. 3, 1975.

Ted Hughes "On Sylvia Plath," *Raritan*, Fall 1994.

Garry M. Leonard "'The Woman Is Perfected. Her Dead Body Wears the Smile of Accomplishment': Sylvia Plath and *Mademoiselle* Magazine," *College Literature*, vol. 19, no. 2, 1992.

Jerry M. Lewis "Looking Back," *Psychiatric Times*, November 2010.

Robert A. Martin "Esther's Dilemma in *The Bell Jar*," *Notes on Contemporary Literature*, January 1991.

Diane Middlebrook "The Enraged Muse," *Times Literary Supplement* (London), October 27–November 1989.

Rebecca Myers-Spiers "Revisiting *The Bell Jar*: Putting Young Girls Under the Lenses of Patriarchy," *Off Our Backs*, July 7, 1999.

Linda W. Wagner "Plath's *The Bell Jar* as Female Bildungsroman," *Women's Studies: An Interdisciplinary Journal*, vol. 12, no. 1, 1986.

Internet Sources

Lisa Belkin "Depression in Teenagers," *Motherlode: Adventures in Parenting*, March 18, 2010. http://parenting.blogs.nytimes.com.

Eilene Zimmer   "Teen Angst Turns Deadly,"
                     Psychology Today, January 1, 2009.
                     www.psychologytoday.com.

Index